Backpackers Songbook

Compiled by Ron Middlebrook

Words and chords to over 200 favorite songs. Guitar and Banjo Chord charts. Transposing chart too, plus helpful hints for the backpacker.

Thanks to veteran backpacker and sometimes guitar player Ken Ward on the cover.

ISBN 978-0-931759-85-7

SAN 683-8022

© 1982 CENTERSTREAM Publishing P.O. Box 17878-Anaheim Hills, CA 92807 U.S.A. Phone/fax(714) 779-9390

FORWARD

Everyone is not going to know all the songs contained in this book. That's O.K. use the chord changes and make up some melodies yourself. If the chords are a bit hard there's a transposing chart to get you in an easier key. Plus guitar and banjo chord charts to find those easy chords.

When you're held up under a tree or in your tent on that rainy day the songs make good reading too. They all have a message and come from the heart. Enjoy!

GUITAR CONTENTS

SONG CONTENTS

TUNING THE GUITAR

GUITAR TUNING

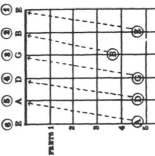

1. Tune the 6th string in unison to the E or twelfth white key to the LEFT of MIDDLE C on the piano.

2. Place the finger behind the fifth fret of the 6th string. This will give you the tone or pitch of the 5th string. (A)

3. Place finger behind the fifth fret of the 5th string to get the pitch of the 4th string. (D)

4. Repeat same procedure to obtain the pitch of the 3d string. (G)

5. Place finger behind the FOURTH FRET of the 3d string to get the pitch of the 2d string. (B)

6. Place finger behind the fifth fret of the 2d string to get the pitch of the 1st string. (E)

7

BANJO FINGERBOARD CHART

G TUNING

NAME OF STRINGS

SHARPS # MOVE UP 1 FRET   FLATS b MOVE BACK 1 FRET

	FRET			
1 D	E	F		G
2 B	C	D		E
3 G		A	B	C
4 D	E	F		G
5 G		A	B	C

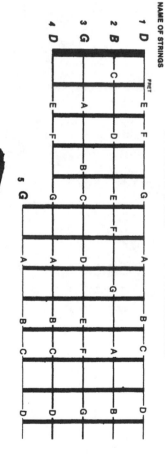

TUNING THE BANJO

The 5 strings are tuned to a piano as shown.

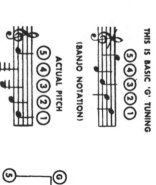

THIS IS BASIC 'G' TUNING

⑤④③②①
(BANJO NOTATION)

⑤④③②①
ACTUAL PITCH

TUNING THE BANJO
TO ITSELF

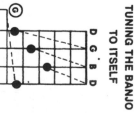

GUITAR FINGERBOARD CHART

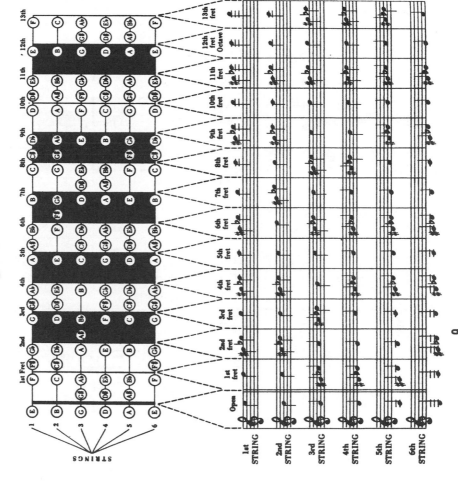

9

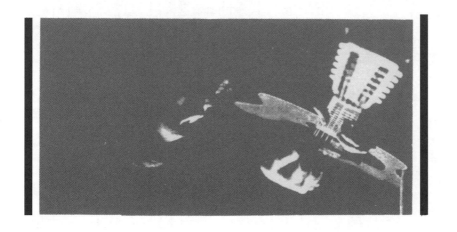

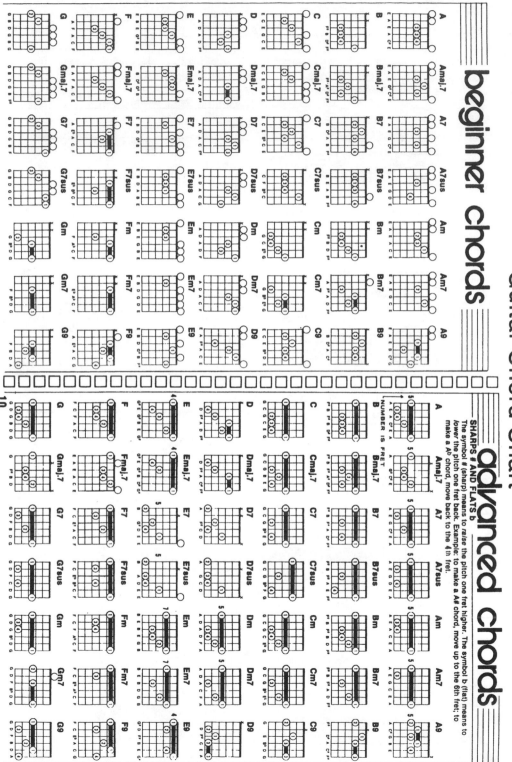

Banjo Chord Chart

FIRST POSITION CHORDS

MAJOR CHORDS

The symbol o above a string means it is to be sounded open

C   D   E   F   G   A

Bb   Eb   Gb or Ab   C# or Db   F# or Gb   B

MINOR CHORDS

Cm   Dm   Em   Fm   Gm   Am

Bbm   Bm   Ebm   F#m   C#m or Dbm   Abm

7th CHORDS

C7 (No Fifth)

In this fingering the fifth string would provide the fifth of the chord.

D7 (No Third)   E7   E7 (No Fifth)   F7

F7   G7   G7   B7 (No Fifth)   B7

MINOR 7 CHORDS

Cm7 no fifth

The fifth string would provide the fifth of the chord.

Em7   Em7   Am7 Five string banjo only   Dm7   Dm7   Gm7

Bm7   Dm7   F#m7

TRANSPOSING CHART

APPLICATION

When you are changing keys, or transposing, the relationship chords to the notes does not change. You are simply moving a song lo... higher to make it easier to play or sing.

1. Locate the Key-note of the song which tells you the key in which you do not want to play.

2. Find the Key-note in the far left column of the Transposing Chart and read across, left to right. Take the Key of "D" as an example:

   D D# E F F# G G# A A# B C C# D

3. Now, draw a line under each chord of the song. Add the type of chord, sevenths, minors, ninths, suspendeds, etc.

   D D# Em7 F F# G G# A7 A# Bm C C# D

4. To find your new Key, look at the far-left column again. Let's pick "G" for your new key. The new chords will appear just below the old chords in the same vertical column.

   D D# Em7 F F# G G# A7 A# Bm C C# D
   G G# Am7 A# B C C# D7 D# Em F F# G

5. Remember your enharmonic equivalents; G# is the same as Ab, F# - Gb, A# - Bb, etc.

6. With this chart you can scan the new key at a glance and see the new chords. The chart works for all types of chords; just be sure to add the additional information on the chords in sevenths, ninths, minors, etc. You can use this chart to transpose the melody notes of songs as well.

7. NOTE: If a C#7 happens to line up in a column with a "G", the chord will be a G7, not a C#7. Don't bring down the sharp which is an interval, rather than a type of chord. If F# lines up with D, that's it. F# is D, not D#.

Key												
A	A#	B	C	C#	D	D#	E	F	F#	G	G#	A
G#	A	A#	B	C	C#	D	D#	E	F	F#	G	G#
G	G#	A	A#	B	C	C#	D	D#	E	F	F#	G
F#	G	G#	A	A#	B	C	C#	D	D#	E	F	F#
F	F#	G	G#	A	A#	B	C	C#	D	D#	E	F
E	F	F#	G	G#	A	A#	B	C	C#	D	D#	E
D#	E	F	F#	G	G#	A	A#	B	C	C#	D	D#
D	D#	E	F	F#	G	G#	A	A#	B	C	C#	D
C#	D	D#	E	F	F#	G	G#	A	A#	B	C	C#
C	C#	D	D#	E	F	F#	G	G#	A	A#	B	C
B	C	C#	D	D#	E	F	F#	G	G#	A	A#	B
A#	B	C	C#	D	D#	E	F	F#	G	G#	A	A#
A	A#	B	C	C#	D	D#	E	F	F#	G	G#	A

PRINCIPLE CHORDS

There are three principle chords in every key. The principle chords are worth knowing as a guide in searching out the chords of a progression. If a song is in the Key of "G" the main or most important chord in that song will be G (called the Tonic or I Chord). The second most important chord will be the D7 (called the dominant or V7 Chord). The third most important chord is the C (called the sub-dominant or IV Chord).

A thorough memorization of these three principle chords (I, IV, V7) is important for developing your ear-playing and a feel for music.

Key	3 Principal Chords			Relative Minor		
C	C	F	G7	Am	Dm	E7
G	G	C	D7	Em	Am	B7
D	D	G	A7	Bm	Em	F#7
A	A	D	E7	F#m	Bm	C#7
E	E	A	B7	C#m	F#m	G#7
B	B	E	F#7	G#m	C#m	D#7
F#	F#	B	C#7	D#m	G#m	A#7
F	F	Bb	C7	Dm	Gm	A7
Bb	Bb	Eb	F7	Gm	Cm	D7
Eb	Eb	Ab	Bb7	Cm	Fm	C7
Ab	Ab	Db	Eb7	Fm	Bbm	G7
Db	Db	Gb	Ab7	Bbm	Ebm	F7

CRAPPIE, CLOSELY RELATED TO BLUEGILL, ARE USUALLY FOUND IN THE SAME HABITAT. LOOK FOR SUBMERGED TREES AND BRUSH AND FIND BOTH. MINNOWS ARE A FAVORITE BAIT BUT THEY'RE ALSO CAUGHT ON SPECIAL JIGS. NINE INCHES IS A GOOD SIZED CRAPPIE. OH, ITS PRONOUNCED "CROP PEA", ITS

Camp 7 Minicatcher

TIPS FOR THE BACKPACKER

BACKPACKER'S DISEASE or BEAVER FEVER

GIARDIA LAMBLIA is the most common pathogenic intestenal parasite in the United States today. Symptoms appear from one to three weeks after ingestion and include diarrhea, abdominal bloating, gas, appetite and weight loss, and nausea sometimes accompanied by fever, headache, gastric cramps and itching, in short, it may not kill, but it may make you wish you were dead.

How to avoid it? Assume that ALL surface water sources contain Giardia and treating by eather boiling, chemical treatment or filtration. For chemical treatment add the disinfectant, shake the bottle, then lossen the container lid slightly, and shake again to get some of the treated water on the screw cap threads (16,500 cysts fit nicely on the head of a pen), Bleach has the least objectionable taste.

Ways to Make Your Water Safe

Recommended Disinfecting Dosages & Contact Times
Per Quart of Water[a]

Disinfectant	Amount	Contact Time[b]
Household bleach	4 drops	30 minutes
Halazone	5 tablets	30 minutes
Hydroperiodide (known commercially as Globaline, Potable-Aqua, Coughlan's, etc.)	2 tablets	30 minutes
Tincture of iodine (2 %)	10 drops	30 minutes

Notes: (a) Data taken from the U.S. Environmental Protection Agency brochure "Don't Drink the Water" which was based on the research of E.L. Jarroll et al., reported in *The American Journal of Tropical Medicine and Hygiene* (1980).
(b) Double the listed contact time for cold water (less than 41°F). When using disinfectants in tablet form, contact time begins after tablets have dissolved and been thoroughly mixed.

SNOW HAZARDS

Hidden Hazards

A steep snowfield ending at a cliff or boulder field is an obvious hazard. You know what you're getting into before you try it. But remember: Snow is not always that obliging. Some hazards are invisible, or at least hidden to the untrained eye.

Avalanches are the best known, but least understood, of these. We do know this: Snow accumulates in distinct layers, a product of alternating storms and fair weather cycles during the winter. While one layer may be very strong, its attachment to lower layers may be weak. Any additional load — you, for example — or any weakening agent such as water from rain or solar surface melting, may upset the balance and set tons of snow in motion. These weaknesses cannot be predicted simply by looking a' a snowfield. A trained observer may spot them, but even he needs on-site studies to determine conditions beneath that innocuous white surface.

Fortunately, the snows of summer tend toward remarkable stability. The alternating freeze-thaw cycles of spring release the most dangerous snow layers.

When there is fresh snowfall, it is best to travel only during the early morning hours after cold, clear nights have frozen the snow. Although cloudy nights may appear to be cold, the cloud cover may prevent radiant heat loss and the snow may never "set up". Beware when the snow is soft, mushy and water laden. When in doubt, chicken out.

As the day warms, the snow surface thaws and becomes progressively more water laden. Your travel may set a small circle of this mushy surface snow in motion, with you aboard. But these slow-moving "avalanche cushions" are usually safe unless you are just above a cliff

Other Pitfalls

In the spring, forces are at work creating snow voids and hollows in what looks to you like nice, solid snow. Running water is one of those forces. Spring melt increases the runoff and as it flows beneath the snow cover, hollow chambers are formed. Many an unwary hiker has crashed through weak snow layers to a streambed below

Hidden streambeds are normally obvious in open meadows. Because of undermining, the snow surface sags along the path of the watercourse. Cross where there is the least sag and, needless to say, don't overload the snow bridge

On steep mountain slopes the streams can be a real hazard where they roar down gulleys loaded with dense snows from winter avalanches. Bridges here can persist well into summer, and breaking through one means more than an irritating splash in a cold puddle. Unsuspecting hikers have been swept downstream under the snow.

Moats form as snow pulls away from cliffs, rock islands, trees and other stationary objects, stretching the overlying snow. By hiking season, moats formed in a snowfield are generally visible (Earlier in the season, moats formed by cliffs and boulders may still be buried.) The first sign of the hidden voids is a discontinuous crack in the snow.

Route Selection

When a map shows a trail somewhere under that unexpected covering of snow, your tendency is to assume that it is still the right route to follow. Remember: Many trails were designed for late-summer use and the problems caused by winter snows have not been considered. Trails may zigzag their way up avalanche bowls to reach alpine ridges, or they may be cut into steep hillsides to avoid unnecessary detour mileage

Time for Self-Arrest

A hiker loses his balance (1) and falls backward down a steep slope (2). To prevent an uncontrolled slide, he digs his ice axe into the snow (3) and flips over (4 and 5) to get in the proper position (6) for a safe self-arrest. Note that toes dig into the snow to aid in arrest. Also, be certain to keep your head and face clear of the axe head.

WHEN RAIN IS NEAR, NATURE GETS EXCITED. LOOK FOR THESE SIGNALS.

- TREE FROGS CRY

- FISH SWIM NEAR THE SURFACE

- LOW CLOUDS MOVE SWIFTLY

- CLOVER LEAVES FOLD TOGETHER

ALTOCUMULUS — FAIR WEATHER FOR A WHILE.

CIRROCUMULUS — THE MACKEREL SKY; RAIN IS COMING.

CIRROSTRATUS — RINGS AROUND THE SUN AND MOON; A STORM IS NEAR.

CUMULONIMBUS — THUNDERSHOWER CLOUDS.

HEAT EMERGENCIES

HEAT EXHAUSTION. Heat exhaustion-as the name indicates-is caused by heat. It usually hits a person in an overheated room, but may also overtake him in the sun.

The patient's face is pale, with cold sweat on the forehead. Breathing is shallow. The whole body may be clammy from perspiration. Vomiting is common. NOTE: Do not confuse with heat stroke which requires a different kind of first aid.

First Aid. Heat exhaustion may be considered shock from heat. Regular care for shock therefore is in order. Move the patient to a shady, cool spot. Place him on his back. Raise his feet. Loosen his clothing. Fan him or apply cool, wet cloths. Give him sips of salt water: 1 teaspoon salt to 1 glass water.

HEAT STROKE. Heat stroke is usually caused by exposure to sun. It's a life-and-death matter. Get a doctor at once.

The patient's face is like the sun: red, hot, dry. Breathing is slow and noisy. The pulse is rapid and strong. The body skin feels dry and hot. The patient may be unconscious.

First Aid. Get the patient quickly into a cool, shaded spot. Place him on his back with his head and shoulders raised. Undress him immediately down to his underwear. Then set out to cool him-especially his head-with water. Cover him with dripping wet towels, shirts, cloths. Keep him cool by dousing them with water or by wringing them out in cold water from time to time. When the patient's body has cooled, stop treatment for a while to see if it heats up again. If it does, resume cooling. When the patient regains consciousness, let him drink all the water he wants.

COLD EMERGENCIES

FROSTBITE. When you are out skating or skiing, someone in the party may complain of their ears, nose, fingers, or toes feeling numb. Or you may notice that a person's ears, nose or cheeks are looking grayish-white: a sure sign of frostbite.

First Aid. Get the frozen part thawed out. If part of the face is frozen, have the person remove a glove and cover the part with his hand. If a hand is frostbitten, bring it under the armpit next to the skin. Then get the patient into a warm room. Give them a warm drink. Warm the frozen part by holding it in warm-not hot-running water. Or wrap it in a warm blanket. When the frostbitten part is rewarmed tell the patient to exercise the injured finger or toes.

HYPOTHERMIA. When you hear of someone having "died from exposure" or "frozen to death," the killer may actually have been hypothermia: from hypo, low, and thermia, state of heat. It is caused by the body losing more heat than it generates. It occurs when a person is not clothed warmly enough for the air around him. Such a person is further endangered if he is exhausted, wet and exposed to a strong wind as when caught in a rainstorm. Under such conditions the air doesn't have to be below freezing-a moderate air temperature of 40-50 degrees may result in death.

Hypothermia starts with the patient feeling chilly, tired, irritable. If he is not helped at this stage, he will begin to shiver uncontrollably. Soon his shivering becomes violent. He may act irrationally. He may stumble and fall. If the shivering then stops, he is close to death.

First Aid. If you are on a hike or backpacking trip in severe weather and realize that someone in the party shows early symptoms of hypothermia, stop right then and there. Put up a shelter. Strip the patient gently and get him into a dry sleeping bag. A cold sleeping bag won't help much: a rescuer should also strip and get into the sleeping bag to use his warm body to warm the victim's cold body. When the victim begins to recover, give him a hot drink with plenty of sugar and quick-energy candy. Get him under a doctor's care.

NOTE: The body temperature of a swimmer drops steadily in water cooler than himself. The shivering that results is the onset of hypothermia. Get out of the water. Cover up. Exercise to get warm.

16

How to Guard Against Insect Stings

Hornet   Honeybee   Yellow Jacket   Wasp

As warm weather ushers in the insect season, what new therapies are available for people who are allergic to stings?

A new vaccine has been developed to protect people from life-threatening reactions to insect stings. Approved three years ago by the Food and Drug Administration, the vaccine, made from insect venom, is found to be much more effective than previous vaccines. "If a person has been immunized with the new vaccine and is stung again by the same insect, there would be virtually no chance of a severe reaction," says allergy specialist Dr. Martin D. Valentine of Baltimore's Good Samaritan Hospital.

How serious are insect stings?

They can be fatal. Each year an estimated 1 million Americans suffer a serious reaction to an insect sting, and in about 50 cases death results. Doctors fear the toll may be higher because the sudden death brought on by a sting can be mistaken for a fatal heart attack.

What insects are most likely to cause a reaction?

Hornets, honeybees, yellow jackets and wasps. There is a lot of geographic variation: In the mid-Atlantic states, yellow jackets are the main culprits. In agricultural areas, honeybees predominate. In the South Central region and parts of the Southwestern states, paper wasps are the worst offenders.

When a person who hasn't been vaccinated has a reaction, what treatment is recommended?

An immediate injection of adrenaline is essential to block the allergic reaction. A special emergency kit equipped with a loaded syringe can be purchased with a doctor's prescription. If the injection is given as soon as symptoms appear, a severe reaction is unlikely. The kit also includes chewable antihistamine tablets, a tourniquet and alcohol swabs.

Also available by prescription is an automatic injector called the EpiPen. A person simply releases the safety cap and presses the device to the thigh. A dose of adrenaline is automatically injected.

Should the antisting kit be in every family's medicine cabinet?

It is a must for people who have a history of allergic reactions to stings or who have just started a vaccination program. The kit should also be available in public places such as swimming clubs, fire and police stations, recreational areas and summer camps.

Who should get the new vaccine?

Adults over 40 who have had generalized reactions and are found to be allergic to one or more of the venoms on a skin test. In the age group between 15 and 40, doctors generally recommend the vaccine for anyone who has experienced severe symptoms from a sting and has a positive skin test. Below the age of 15, the vaccine is usually reserved only for children who have had a life-threatening reaction. There is new evidence that children with less severe reactions tend to outgrow their allergy to stings.

Why not vaccinate everybody who has had a general allergic reaction?

The immunization process is long and time-consuming. In the initial phase, injections are required once a week until a person reaches a maintenance level. Boosters are given once a month for six months and every six weeks thereafter. Since the vaccine is still fairly new, doctors don't know how long boosters will have to be given to maintain immunity. Preliminary findings from studies with children suggest that boostantihistamine chlorpheniramine, which is available in tablet or liquid form, can help relieve itching and is often effective against hives. Swelling usually disappears within 24 hours.

What's the best way to avoid getting stung?

Some common-sense rules: Avoid activities that are sure to attract insects, such as eating outdoors. Don't go around barefoot. Be careful mowing the lawn, cutting vines and pulling weeds.

Wear neutral-colored clothing and avoid floral prints. A pretty, patterned shirt or blouse can look to an insect like a bunch of flowers. Perfume and hair sprays also tend to attract insects. Trying to shoo insects away tends to aggravate them.

Unfortunately, no repellent has been developed that is effective against stinging insects.

What are the symptoms of a life-threatening reaction?

Loss of consciousness, a drop in blood pressure to undetectable levels and respiratory arrest—the person simply stops breathing. A less severe response involves general swelling of the body, hives, shortness of breath and asthma.

Generally, the quicker the reaction, the more dangerous the sting. Severe reactions can develop within minutes.

Death results from the body's inability to supply blood to the brain or from asphyxiation due to hives in the throat, in the larynx or at the back of the tongue.

emergency
FIRST AID

PART I

THE FIVE BASIC STEPS

STEP ONE

SEND SOMEONE FOR HELP. Don't *you* go, unless absolutely essential. You're needed to help the victim. Tell the person to call the emergency number for your area (you should record all emergency phone numbers on the back cover of this booklet), or the operator. Give your messenger as much information as possible without causing extensive delay, and tell him to pass everything along.

STEP TWO

DON'T MOVE THE VICTIM. The only exceptions are when the victim would be in further danger if not moved immediately, such as a car accident where there is danger of gasoline explosion. Otherwise, leave him alone. You risk aggravating any injuries by improper moving. Wait until trained rescuers arrive.

STEP THREE

CHECK FOR BREATHING AND HEART-BEAT. Put your ear to his face and listen, and at the same time watch for the rise and fall of his chest. (See Fig. 1) If the victim is breathing, his heart is beating. *If he's not breathing*, blow four quick breaths into his mouth, then check his pulse by putting your finger on his neck, just to the side of his Adam's apple. (See Fig. 2) Feel for a pulse for 10 seconds. *If*

Fig. 1: *Check for breathing.*

you're sure there is no pulse, begin cardiopulmonary resuscitation.

If his heart is beating but he's still not breathing, continue mouth-to-mouth resuscitation.

Fig. 2: *Feel for a pulse.*

STEP FOUR

CHECK FOR BLEEDING. The best way to stop bleeding is by applying a sterile bandage or other wound dressing, or the cleanest piece of cloth that's available. Hold the dressing in place with your hand. (See Fig. 3) Once applied, don't remove it. If that's not enough to stop the bleeding, raise the affected area above the heart. If *that's* not enough, apply pressure with your fingers to a pressure point. (See Fig. 4 & 5) Do NOT use a tourniquet—they are rarely necessary and can create serious problems.

Fig. 3: *Apply a sterile dressing.*

Fig. 4: *Pressure point on arm . . . .*

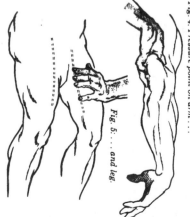

Fig. 5: *. . . and leg.*

STEP FIVE

TREAT FOR SHOCK. Any person who's been injured can be in shock. The treatment consists of keeping the person lying down and as calm as possible. Make sure he's breathing, elevate the legs slightly (unless he has a head injury or fractured leg), and keep him warm, but not hot. Don't give any liquids.

MOUTH-TO-MOUTH RESUSCITATION

When someone stops breathing, no matter whether it happened because of drowning, electrical shock, heart attack, or anything else, you can breathe for him by giving mouth-to-mouth resuscitation. Here's how:

1. Place victim on his back.

2. Check inside the mouth for material that could block the air passage. Clean out if necessary.

3. Kneeling at the side of his head, place one hand on the forehead and the other under his neck. Tilt the head back (unless you suspect a neck injury) so the jaw is pointed up. This keeps the airway open.

4. With the hand that's on the forehead, pinch the nostrils shut.

5. Blow four quick breaths into victim's mouth, hard enough to fill

Fig. 6: Blow into victim's mouth.

lungs. (See Fig. 6) If chest doesn't rise, clear the airway by cleaning out mouth, or roll victim on his side and slap between shoulder blades to dislodge material. Then roll him back and try breathing again.

6. After the four initial breaths, remove your mouth and watch for chest to fall.

7. Continue by blowing one breath into victim's mouth every five seconds until he starts breathing again on his own. (For small children, blow into mouth and nose, one breath every three seconds.)

CPR is the only way to save the life of someone whose heart has stopped. To learn it properly, you should take a CPR course. The American Heart Association and the American Red Cross offer excellent CPR courses.

If you've determined that a person has no heartbeat (step three,   you must begin CPR. Here's how:

1. Kneel at the person's side.

2. Find the bottom of his breastbone—the bone in the middle of the chest.

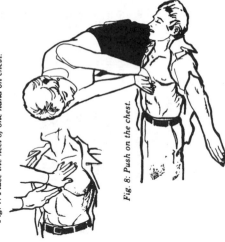

Fig. 7: Place the heel of one hand on chest.

Fig. 8: Push on the chest.

19

3. About two inches above that, place the heel of one hand. (See Fig. 7)

4. Place your other hand over the first hand and lock the fingers.

5. With arms kept straight, push down on the chest, so that it's compressed about 1-1/2 or 2 inches. YOU MUST PUSH FAIRLY HARD. (See Fig. 8)

6. As you push, count out loud: "One, and two, and three, and four, and ....." Keep going a little faster than one push per second, till you get to 15.

7. After 15 pushes, move quickly back to the person's head, and blow two quick breaths into his mouth.

8. Then go right back to his chest, find the spot two inches above the bottom of the breastbone again, place your hands, and push 15 times again.

9. Keep on with 15 pushes, then two breaths, and so on, until one of these things happens:

a. You are relieved by someone who can do CPR, or

b. The person's heart starts beating (check his pulse every minute or so). You may still have to continue mouth-to-mouth resuscitation. Or,

c. A doctor pronounces the person dead.

PART II

HEART ATTACK

How to recognize one

Some or all of these symptoms can point to a heart attack:

1. Pain, usually in the middle of the chest, or the left shoulder and arm, or the neck. May feel like a crushing force.

2. Pale and sweaty skin.

3. Feeling of impending doom.

4. Shortness of breath.

What to do

1. First follow The Five Basic Steps.

2. If victim is conscious, keep him as calm as possible in whatever position is most comfortable. Loosen tight clothing. No liquids. Wait for ambulance to arrive.

3. If victim is unconscious, monitor breathing and heartbeat.

4. If breathing or heartbeat stops, administer mouth-to-mouth resuscitation or CPR, as appropriate.

AUTO ACCIDENTS

1. Your safety comes first. Don't do anything that will risk your own life (e.g., stopping your car on a busy highway).

2. Don't move anyone unless there is imminent danger of explosion, further collision, or unless CPR must be performed.

3. Complete The Five Basic Steps.

4. If there is more than one victim, treat the person with the most serious injuries first.

5. Don't try to do more than you know how. It's better to wait for trained rescue personnel to arrive. But by all means, do what you can.

ELECTRIC SHOCK

1. Break the circuit. Either unplug the appliance, or separate the victim from the source of current, but ONLY with extreme caution. Use a dry, nonmetallic object, such as a wooden pole, a rope, a piece of wooden furniture.

2. Complete The Five Basic Steps.

3. If the victim is burned, follow the procedure on page

POISONING

If you suspect someone has swallowed a poison, or an overdose of something not normally poisonous, assume the worst and follow this procedure:

1. Complete The Five Basic Steps.

2. Try to find out what the person swallowed. Call the nearest hospital or Poison Control Center. (Record the number on back cover of this booklet.) Follow their instructions. If unable to contact help, proceed as follows.

3. If the victim is conscious, dilute the poison by giving him a glass of water or milk.

4. If you know what the antidote is (it may be specified on the container), give the antidote.

5. If unable to give the antidote, induce vomiting, EXCEPT in these cases: corrosives, such as lye or acid; or petroleum products, such as gasoline or paint thinner. The best way to make someone throw up is by giving him a half-ounce of *syrup of ipecac* and a glass of water. Ipecac is available without a prescription at any drugstore.

CHOKING

How to recognize

Someone who's choking won't be able to utter a sound. He may also clutch at his throat.

What to do

1. Stand behind the victim, and support him in front. Bend him forward and slap him soundly between the shoulder blades to dislodge material from his throat.

2. If that doesn't work, use the Heimlich Maneuver:

   a. Wrap your arms around the victim's waist from behind.

   b. Make a fist and put it, thumb in, against the victim's stomach, between the belly button and ribs.

   c. Grab the fist with the other hand and pull sharply in and up. If necessary, repeat several times. (See Fig. 10)

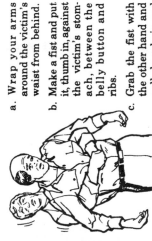

Fig. 10: Heimlich Maneuver.

3. Complete The Five Basic Steps.

BROKEN BONES

How to recognize

If you're in doubt about whether someone has broken bones, assume that he has.

What to do

1. Complete The Five Basic Steps.

2. Keep the victim calm and still.

3. If it becomes absolutely essential to move the person, or you cannot keep him still, you should splint the fracture with whatever suitable material is available. You can use branches, boards, rolled newspapers, or even the body itself (e.g., tie broken leg to uninjured one). For a broken ankle, carefully wrap the foot in a pillow, and tie it closed. For any fracture, don't tie anything directly over the wound—tie the above and below it. (See Fig. 9) Best procedure, though, is to wait for trained rescuers to arrive, if you can.

Fig. 9: Rolled newspaper splint.

6. If the poison was carbon monoxide, get the person to fresh air immediately, monitor breathing, and wait for help.

7. If the poison is from a snakebite, keep victim calm, monitor breathing, and wait for help.

BURNS

Burns are caused by fire, hot liquids, chemicals, electricity, and even by excessive exposure to the sun. The basic treatment is the same for all.

1. Complete The Five Basic Steps.

2. To minimize the risk of infection, do not touch the burned area and do not remove burned clothing that's stuck to the skin. Immerse the burned area in (or flush it with) cold water.

3. If help will arrive soon, don't cover the wound. If not, cover with a loose, sterile dressing or anything clean, such as a sheet.

4. No ointments or salves.

5. Give nothing to drink.

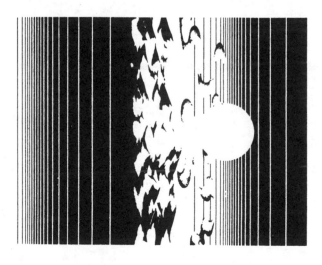

A Horse Named Bill
Tune: *Dixie*

C
I had a horse, his name was Bill,
F   G7
And when he ran he couldn't stand still,
   C
He ran away one day,
  G7   C
And also I ran with him.

He ran so hard he couldn't stop.
He ran into a barber shop.
He fell exhausted with his teeth
In the barber's left shoulder.

O, I went out into the woods last year
To hunt for beer and not for deer
I am I ain't
A great sharpshooter.

At shooting birds I am a beaut.
There is no bird I cannot shoot
In the eye in the ear
In the finger.

In Frisco Bay there lives a whale
And she eats pork chops by the bale
By the hatbox, by the pillbox
By the hogshead, and schooner.

Her name in Lena, she is a peach
But don't leave food within her reach
Or babies or nursemaids
Or chocolate ice cream sodas.

America The Beautiful
Katherine Lee Bates and Samuel A. Ward

  C   G7
Oh beautiful for spacious skies,
            C
For amber waves of grain,
G7 C   G
For purple mountain majesties
     D7   G
Above the fruited plain.
G7C   G7
America! America!
            C
God shed His grace on thee,
C7 F   C
And crown thy good with brotherhood
     F   G7   C
From sea to shining sea.

She loves to laugh and when she smiles
You just see teeth for miles and miles
And tonsils and spareribs
And things too fierce to mention.

She knows no games so when she plays
She rolls her eyes for days and days
She vibrates and yodels
And breaks the Ten Commandments.

O, what can you do in a case like that
O, what can you do but stamp on your hat
Or on an eggshell or a toothbrush
Or anything that's helpless.

Oh beautiful for pilgrim feet
Whose stern impassioned stress
A thoroughfare for freedom beat
Across the wilderness.
America! America!
God mend thine every flaw,
Confirm thy soul in self-control,
Thy liberty in law.

Oh beautiful for heroes proved
In liberating strife,
Who more than self their country loved
And mercy more than life.
America! America!
May God thy gold refine
Till all success be nobleness,
And every gain divine.

Oh beautiful for patriot dream
That sees beyond the years,
Thine alabaster cities gleam,
Undimmed by human tears.
America! America!
God shed His grace on thee,
And crown thy good with brotherhood
From sea to shining sea.

Shoe Fly
(eating shoofly pie)

Alouette

France

Alouette

G   D7   G
Alouette, gentille Alouette
D7   G
Alouette, je te plumerai.

D7   G
Je te plumerai la tête,
D7   G
Je te plumerai la tête;
D7
Et la tête, et la tête, Oh . . .
Et le bec (et le bec),
Et la tête (et la tête, Oh, etc.)

Le nez

Le dos

Les jambes

Les pieds

Les pattes

Le cou

The Arkansas Traveler

D   E   D
Oh, once upon a time in Arkansas,
G   D   G   A7
An old man sat in his little cabin door,
D   G   A7   D
And fiddled at a tune that he liked to hear,
G   A7   D
A jolly old tune that he played by ear.

Em   D   A7
I was raining hard, but the fiddler didn't care,
D   A   D   A
He sawed away at the popular air,
D   Em   D   A7
Though his rooftop leaked like a waterfall,
D   G   D   A7 D
That didn't seem to bother the old man at all.

A traveler was riding by that day,
And stopped to hear him a-fiddling away;
The cabin was afloat and his feet were wet,
But the old man still didn't seem to fret.
So the stranger said, "Now, the way it seems to me,
You'd better mend your roof," said he,
But the old man said as he played away:
"I couldn't mend it now, it's a rainy day."

The traveler replied, "That's all quite true,
But this, I think, is the thing for you to do;
Get busy on a day that is fair and bright,
Then patch the old roof till it's good and tight."
But the old man kept on a-playing at his reel,
And tapped the ground with his leathery heel:
"Get along," said he, "for you give me a pain;
My cabin never leaks when it doesn't rain!"

Aunt Rhody

D
Go tell Aunt Rhody,
G   A7   D
That the old gray goose is dead.
A7   D
The one she's been saving (3 times)
To make a feather bed.

D
Go tell Aunt Rhody,
A7
Go tell Aunt Rhody,

G   A7   D
Old gander's weeping (3 times)
Because his wife is dead.

And the goslings are mourning (3 times)
Because their mother's dead.

She died in the mill-pond (3 times)
Standing on her head.

24

Barbara Allen

Child Ballad 84

E
In Scarlet Town where I was born,
      B7
There was a fair maid dwelling,
E
Made many a youth cry well a day,
     B   E
Her name was Barbara Allen.

It was in the merry month of May
When green buds they were swelling;
Sweet William came from the west country
And he courted Barbara Allen.

He sent his servant unto her
To the place where she was dwelling;
Said my master's sick, bids me call for you
If your name be Barbara Allen.

Well, slowly, slowly got she up
And slowly went she nigh him;
But all she said as she passed his bed
Young man I think you're dying.

Then lightly tripped she down the stairs
She heard those church bells tolling;
And each bell seemed to say as it tolled
Hard-hearted Barbara Allen.

O, mother, mother go make my bed
And make it long and narrow;
Sweet William died for me today
I'll die for him tomorrow.

They buried Barbara in the old church yard
They buried Sweet William beside her;
Out of his grave grew a red, red rose
And out of hers a briar.

They grew and grew up the old church wall
Till they could grow no higher;
And at the top twined in a lovers' knot
The red rose and the briar.

Beautiful Brown Eyes

Chorus:

C   F
Beautiful, beautiful brown eyes,
C   G7
Beautiful, beautiful brown eyes,
C   F
Beautiful, beautiful brown eyes,
    G7   C
I'll never see blue eyes again.

Willie, my darling, I love you,
Love you with all of my heart;
Tomorrow we were to be married,
But liquor has kept us apart.

I staggered into the barroom,
I fell down on the floor,
And the very last words that I uttered,
"I'll never get drunk any more."

Seven long years I've been married,
I wish I was single again,
A woman don't know half her troubles
Until she has married a man.

Bill Groggin's Goat

G
There was a man (there was a man),
        C
Now please take note (now please take note),
        D7
There was a man (there was a man)
        G
Who had a goat (who had a goat).

He loved that goat (he loved that goat),
        C
Indeed he did (indeed he did),
        D7
He loved that goat (he loved that goat)
        G
Just like a kid (just like a kid).

One day the goat, etc.
Felt frisk and fine, etc.
Ate three red shirts, etc.
Right off the line, etc.
The man, he grabbed, etc.
Him by the back, etc.
And tied him to, etc.
A railroad track., etc.

Now when that train, etc.
Hove into sight, etc.
That goat grew pale, etc.
And green with fright, etc.
He heaved a sigh, etc.
As if in pain, etc.
Coughed up the shirts, etc.
And flagged the train., etc.

25

Bile Them Cabbage Down

A
Went up on the mountain
         E7
Just to give my horn a blow,
A   D
Thought I heard my true love say,
A   E7   A
"Yonder comes my beau!"

Chorus:

A   D
Bile them cabbage down, down,
A   E7
Turn them hoecakes round,
         A   D
The only song that I can sing
A   E7   A
Is bile them cabbage down.

A
Took my gal to the blacksmith shop
To have her mouth made small
She turned around a time or two
And swallowed shop and all.

Possum in a 'simmon tree,
Raccoon on the ground,
Raccoon says, "You son-of-a-gun,
Shake some 'simmons down!"

Met a possum in the road,
Blind as he could be,
Jumped the fence and whipped my dog
And bristled up at me.

Once I had an old gray mule,
His name was Simon Slick,
He'd roll his eyes and back his ears,
And how that mule would kick.

How that mule would kick!
He kicked with his dying breath;
He shoved his hind feet down his throat
And kicked himself to death.

Someone stole my old 'coon dog,
Wish they'd bring him back,
He chased the big hogs through the fence
And the little ones through the crack.

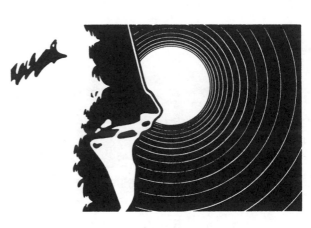

Beautiful Dreamer

Stephen Foster

C   Dm
Beautiful dreamer, wake unto me,
G7   C
Starlight and dewdrops are waiting for thee.
                                   Dm
Sounds of the rude world heard in the day,
G7   C
Lulled by the moonlight have all passed away.
G7   C
Beautiful dreamer, queen of my song,
Am   D7   G7
List while I woo thee with soft melody.
C   Dm
Gone are the cares of life's busy throng,
G7   C   E7   Am
Beautiful dreamer, awake unto me,
F   C   G7   C
Beautiful dreamer, awake unto me.

Beautiful dreamer, out on the sea
Mermaids are chanting the wild Lorelei;
Over the streamlet vapors are borne
Waiting to fade at the bright coming morn.
Beautiful dreamer, beam on my heart
E'en as the morn on the streamlet and sea,
Then will all clouds of sorrow depart.
Beautiful dreamer, awake unto me,
Beautiful dreamer, awake unto me.

The Battle Hymn Of The Republic

Julia Ward Howe/Tune: *John Brown's Body*

G
Mine eyes have seen the glory of the coming of the Lord;
    C
He is trampling out the vintage
    G
where the grapes of wrath are stored;

He hath loosed the fateful lightning
  G B7   Em
of His terrible swift sword,
  Am   G   D7 G
His truth is marching on.

Chorus:

G
Glory, Glory, Hallelujah,
C   G
Glory, Glory, Hallelujah,
           GEm
Glory, Glory, Hallelujah
  Am   G   D7 G
His truth is marching on.

I have seen him in the watch fires
of a hundred circling camps;
They have builded him an altar
in the evening dews and damps;
I can read his righteous sentence
by the dim and flaring lamps,
His day is marching on.

I have read a fiery gospel writ in burnished rows of steel:
"As ye deal with My contemners,
so with you My Grace shall deal;
Let the Hero, born of woman,
crush the serpent with his heel,
Since God is marching on.

He has sounded for the trumphet
that shall never call retreat;
He is sifting out the hearts of men
before His Judgement Seat;
Oh! Be swift, my soul, to answer Him,
be jubilant, my feet!
Our God is marching on.

In the beauties of the lilies Christ was born across the sea,
With a glory in his bosom that transfigures you and me;
As He died to make men holy, let us die to make men free,
While God is marching on.

Black-Eyed Susie

G   D7
All I want in this creation
G   C
Pretty little wife and a big plantation.

Chorus:

G   C   D7
Hey, little black-eyed Susie,
G   C   D7
Hey, little black-eyed Susie,
G   C   D7 G
Hey, little black-eyed Susie, hey!

All I need to keep me happy,
Two little boys to call me pappy.

Up Red Oak and down salt water,
Some old man gonna lose his daughter.

Black-eyed Susie went huckleberry pickin',
The boys got drunk and Susie took a lickin'.

Some got drunk and some got boozy,
I went home with black-eyed Susie.

Black-eyed Susie about half-grown,
Jumps on the boys like a dog on a bone.

I asked her to be my wife,
She come at me with a barlow knife.

Love my wife, love my baby,
Love my biscuits sopped in gravy.

Black Is The Color

```
             Am           D
Black is the color of my true love's hair,
     Am    D    Am  D
Her lips are like some rosy fair;
     Am    D    Am  D Am    D
I'll write to you in a few short lines,
I'll suffer death ten thousand times.

The purest eyes and the neatest hands,
          Am        D
I love the ground where-on she stands.

          Am             D
I go to the Clyde for to mourn and weep,
But satisfied I never can sleep,
I'll write to you in a few short lines,
I'll suffer death ten thousand times.

I know my love and well she knows
I love the grass whereon she goes,
If she on earth no more I see,
My life will quickly fade away.

A winter's past and the leaves are green,
The time has passed that we have seen,
But still I hope the time will come
When you and I will be as one.
```

Blood On The Saddle

```
            D
There was blood on the saddle
     G        D
And blood on the ground,
        A7       D
And a great big puddle
     A7     D
Of blood all around.

The cowboy lay in it,
All covered with gore,
And he won't go riding
No broncos no more.

Oh, pity the cowboy,
All bloody and red,
For his bronco fell on him
And mashed in his head.
```

Blow The Man Down

Chorus:
```
D                 D6        D           D6
Oh blow the man down bullies, Blow the man down,
     D    D6  Em        A7
To me way! hey! Blow the man down,
Em              A7      Em
Oh, Blow the man down bullies, Blow him away,
A7                    D
Give me some time to blow the man down.
```

```
As I was a-walkin' down Paradise Street,
To me way! hey!—Blow the man down!
A pretty young damsel I chanced for to meet,
Give me some time to blow the man down.

She hailed me with her flipper, I took her in tow,
To me way! hey!—Blow the man down!
Yard-arm to yard-arm away we did go
Give me some time to blow the man down.

As soon as that Packet was clear of the bar,
To me way! hey!—Blow the man down!
The mate knocked me down with the end of a spar,
Give me some time to blow the man down.

Its yard-arm to yard-arm away you will sprawl,
Way! hey!—Blow the man down!
For kicking Jack Rogers commands the Black Ball
Give me some time to blow the man down.
```

Clementine

E
In a cavern, in a canyon,
    B7
Excavating for a mine,
    E
Lived a miner, forty niner,
    B7   E
And his daughter, Clementine.

Chorus:
E
Oh, my darling, Oh, my darling,
              B7
Oh, my darling, Clementine,
        E
You are lost and gone forever,
    B7   E
Dreadful sorry, Clementine.

Light she was and, like a fairy,
And her shoes were number nine,
Herring boxes, without topses,
Sandals were for Clementine.

Drove she ducklings to the water,
Every morning just at nine,
Stubbed her toe upon a splinter,
Fell into the foaming brine.

Ruby lips above the water,
Blowing bubbles soft and fine,
But alas I was no swimmer,
So I lost my Clementine.

There's a churchyard, on the hillside,
Where the flowers grow and twine,
There grow roses, 'mongst the posies,
Fertilized by Clementine.

Brigham Young

        A
Brigham Young was a Mormon bold,
    E   A
And a leader of the roaring ram,
              D
And the shepherd of a flock of fine tub sheep
  A   E   A
And a passel of pretty little lambs;
    E   A
And he lived with his five and forty wives
              D
In the city of the Great Salt Lake,
Where they breed and swarm like hens on a farm
    A   E   A
And cackle like ducks to a drake.

Chorus:
A
Brigham Young, Brigham Young,
    E   A
It's a miracle he survived,
              D
With his roaring rams, and his pretty little lambs,
    A   E   A
And his five and forty wives.

Number forty-five's about sixteen,
Number one is sixty and three,
And among such a riot how he ever keeps 'em quiet
Is a downright mystery to me,
For they cackle and claw and they jaw, jaw, jaw, jaw,
Each one has a different desire,
It would aid the renown of the best shop in town
To supply them with half they require.

Brigham Young was a stout man once,
But now he is thin and old,
And I'm sorry to relate, there's no hair upon his pate,
Where he once wore a covering of gold.
For his oldest wife won't wear white wool,
The young ones won't take red,
And in tearing it out and taking turn about,
They have torn all the wool from his head.

Chewing Gum

F   C7
Mama sent me to the spring,
                F
She told me not to stay,
                       C7
Fell in love with a pretty little girl,
           F
Could not get away.

Chorus:

F   C7   F
Chewing chewing gum, chewing chawing gum,
               C7   F
Chawing chewing gum, chewing chawing gum.

First she gave me peaches nice,
Then she gave me pears,
Next she gave me 50 cents,
She kissed me on the stairs.

I wouldn't have a lawyer,
Now here's the reason why,
Every time he opens his mouth,
He tells a great big lie.

I wouldn't have a doctor,
Now here's the reason why,
He rides all over the country,
A-making the people die.

I took my girl to the church last night,
And what do you reckon she done,
She walked right up to the preacher's face
And chawed her chewing gum.

Cripple Creek

D   G   D
I got a gal and she loves me,
      A7   D
She's as sweet as sweet can be.
            G   D
She's got eyes of baby blue,
           A7   D
Makes my gun shoot straight and true.

Chorus:

D   G6
Goin' down Cripple Creek,
D
Goin' in a run,
            G6
Goin' down Cripple Creek
D   Em   D
To 'ave some fun.

I got a beau and he loves me,
He's as sweet as sweet can be.
He's got eyes of darkest brown,
Makes my heart jump all around!

Mama don't 'low me to whistle,
Poppa don't 'low me to sing,
They don't want me to marry,
I'll marry just the same.

Columbus Stockade Blues

      E
Way down in Columbus, Georgia,
B7   E
Want to go back to Tennessee.
            E
Way down in Columbus Stockade,
     B7
My friends all turned their backs on me.

Chorus: A   E
Well, you can go and leave if you want to.
A   B7
Never let it cross your mind,
         E
For in your heart you love another,
B7   E
Leave, little darlin', I don't mind.

Last night as I lay sleeping,
I dreamed I held you in my arms,
When I woke, I was mistaken,
I was peeping through the bars.

Many hours with you I've rambled,
Many nights with you I've spent alone,
Now you've gone, you've gone and left me,
And broken up our happy home.

The Blue-Tail Fly

    A
When I was young I used to wait
E   **B7**
On master and serve him his plate,
   A
And pass the bottle when he got dry,
B7   **E**
And brush away the blue-tail fly.

Chorus:

       B7
Jimmy crack corn and I don't care.
      E
Jimmy crack corn and I don't care.
      A
Jimmy crack corn and I don't care,
B7   **E**
My master's gone away.

And when he'd ride in the afternoon
I'd follow with a hickory broom,
The pony being rather shy
When bitten by the blue-tail fly.

One day he rode around the farm
The flys so numerous they did swarm,
One chanced to bite him on the thigh
The devil take a blue-tail fly.

The pony jump, he toss, he pitch
He threw my master in the ditch,
He died and the jury wondered why
The verdict was the blue-tail fly.

Careless Love

  E   **B7**   **E**
Love, oh, oh, oh careless love,
              B7
Love, oh, oh, love, oh careless love,
E   **E7** **A**
Love, oh, oh, love, oh careless love,
      E   **B7**   **E**
You see what love has done to me.

I love my mama and papa too, (3 times)
I'd leave them both to go with you.

What, oh what, will mama say, (3 times)
When she learns I've gone astray.

Once I wore my apron low, (3 times)
I couldn't scarcely keep you from my door.

Now my apron strings don't pin, (3 times)
You pass my door and you don't come in.

House Fly

He lies beneath a 'simmon tree
His epitaph is there to see,
Beneath this stone I'm forced to lie
The victim of a blue-tail fly.

Camptown Races
Stephen Foster

C
Oh, the Camptown ladies sing this song,
G7
Doo-da, doo-da,
      C
The Camptown race track's two miles long,
G7   **C**
Oh, de doo-da day.

Chorus:

C
Goin' to run all night,
F   **C**
Goin' to run all day,

I bet my money on a bob-tailed nag,
G7   **C**
Somebody bet on the bay.

Oh, the long tailed filly and the big big black horse,
Doo-da, doo-da,
Come to a mud hole and they all cut across,
Oh, de doo-da day.

I went down South with my hat caved in,
Doo-da, doo-da,
I come back North with a pocket full of tin,
Oh, de doo-da day.

31

Bury Me Not On The Lone Prairie

Em   G
"Oh, bury me not on the lone prairie,"
     Em
Those words came low and mournfully
      G
From the pallid lips of a youth who lay
      Bm   Em
 G   A   C   D
On his dying bed at the close of day.

Chorus:

    G   D7   G
"Oh, bury me not on the lone prairie,
                D7   Em
Where the wild coyotes will howl o'er me,
   G   D7   Bm
In a narrow grave just six by three.
  C   D6 D7 G
Oh, bury me not on the lone prairie.

       G   D7   G
"It matters not, I've oft been told,
Where the body lies when the heart grows cold.
   G   D7   Em
Yet grant, oh grant, this wish to me:
Oh, bury me not on the lone prairie.

"I've always wished to be laid when I died
In the little churchyard on the green hillside;
By my father's grave there let mine be,
And bury me not on the lone prairie.

"Let my death-slumber be where my mother's prayer
And a sister's tear will mingle there;
Where my friends can come and weep o'er me.
Oh bury me not on the lone prairie."

"Oh, bury me not"—and his voice failed there,
But we took no heed of his dying prayer.
In a narrow grave just six by three
We buried him on the lone prairie.

And the cowboys now as they roam the plain,
For they marked the spot where his bones were lain,
Fling a handful of roses o'er the grave
With a prayer to Him who his soul will save.

"Oh, bury me not on the lone prairie,
Where the wolves can howl and growl o'er me.
Fling a handful of roses o'er my grave
With a prayer to Him who my soul will save."

32

Comin' Through The Rye

G   D7
Gin a body meet a body,
G   D7   G
Comin' through the rye,
        D7
Gin a body kiss a body,
G   D7 G
         D7
Need a body cry?
           D7
Ilka lassie has her laddie,
G7   C
Nane, they say, hae I,
      G   D7   G   D
Yet a' the lads they smile at me,
       G   D7   G
When comin' through the rye.

Gin a body meet a body,
Comin' frae the toon,
Gin a body greet a body,
Need a body froon?

Among the train there is a swain,
I dearly love mysel',
But what's his name or what's his hame,
I donna care to tell.

Cindy

```
G
You ought to see my Cindy,

She lives way down south;

She's so sweet the honey bees
D7        G
Swarm around her mouth.
```

Chorus:

```
      C
Get along home, Cindy, Cindy,
      G
Get along home, Cindy, Cindy,
      C
Get along home, Cindy, Cindy,
      D7        G
I'll marry you some day.
```

```
The first I seen my Cindy
She was standing in the door,
Her shoes and stockings in her hand,
Her feet all over the floor.
```

```
She took me to her parlor,
She cooled me with her fan;
She said I was the prettiest thing
In the shape of mortal man.
```

```
She kissed me and she hugged me,
She called me sugar plum;
She throwed her arms around me,
I thought my time had come.
```

Londonderry Air

```
         G                              C
Oh son of mine, the valley seems so empty.
                          G           Am7 D7
The shouts of Spring have fallen to a sigh,
                                  G                      C
When Winter comes, I'm  sure  that  it  will  claim-me,
D7 Am7 D7 G            D7 G
For why's to live, when there is but to die.
```

```
But 'til the sun has fallen like an ember.
And 'til the wind is heavy with the rain.
I will relive each moment that we had of you.
And pray to God you were not called to death in vain.
```

```
Oh, Cindy is a pretty girl,
Cindy is a peach.
She threw her arms around my neck,
And hung on like a leech.
```

```
And if I was a sugar tree
Standing in the town,
Every time my Cindy passed
I'd shake some sugar down.
```

```
And if I had a thread and needle
Fine as I could sew,
I'd sew that gal to my coat tails
And down the road I'd go.
```

```
I wish I was an apple
A-hanging on a tree,
Every time that Cindy passed.
She'd take a bite of me.
```

Cumberland Gap

```
F                    Dm
Lay down boys, take a little nap,
            F
We're all goin' down to Cumberland Gap.
                              Dm
Cumberland Gap, Cumberland Gap.
     F         G7      F
We're all goin' down to Cumberland Gap.
```

```
Me and my wife, and my wife's pap
We all live down to Cumberland Gap.
Cumberland Gap, Cumberland Gap
We all live down to Cumberland Gap.
```

```
I got a gal in Cumberland Gap,
She's got a baby calls me pap.
Cumberland Gap, Cumberland Gap
We're all going down to Cumberland Gap.
```

```
Cumberland Gap it ain't very fur,
It's just three miles from Middlesboro, etc.
```

33

Crawdad

E
You get a line and I'll get a pole, honey,
          B7
You get a line and I'll get a pole, babe.
E   E7
You get a line and I'll get a pole,
   A7
And we'll go down to the Crawdad hole,
E   B7   E
Honey, sugar baby, mine,

Get up old man, you slept too late, honey, (twice)
Get up old man, you slept too late,
Last piece of crawdad's on your plate,
Honey, sugar baby mine.

Get up old woman, you slept too late, honey, (twice)
Get up old woman, you slept too late,
Crawdad man done passed your gate,
Honey, sugar baby mine.

Along come a man with a sack on his back, honey, (twice)
Along come a man with a sack on his back,
Packin' all the crawdads he can pack,
Honey, sugar baby mine.

What you gonna do when the lake goes dry, (twice)
What you gonna do when the lake goes dry,
Sit on the bank and watch the crawdads die,
Honey, sugar baby mine.

What you gonna do when the crawdads die, honey?
  (twice)

What you gonna do when the crawdads die,
Sit on the bank until I cry,
Honey, sugar baby mine.

I heard the duck say to the drake, honey, (twice)
I heard the duck say to the drake,
There ain't no crawdads in this lake,
Honey, sugar baby mine.

Cotton-Eyed Joe

A   D
Do you remember a long time ago,
A   E7
There was a man called Cotton-Eyed Joe,
     E   A   E   A
There was a man called Cotton-Eyed Joe.

I could have been married a long time ago,
If it hadn't a-been for Cotton-Eyed Joe, (twice)

Old bull fiddle and a shoe-string bow,
Wouldn't play nothin' but Cotton-Eyed Joe, (twice)

Play it fast or play it slow,
Didn't play nothin' but Cotton-Eyed Joe, (twice)

Don't you remember a long time ago,
Daddy worked a man called Cotton-Eyed Joe, (twice)

Where you you come from? where do you go?
Where do you come from Cotton-Eyed Joe? (twice)

Come for to see you, come for to sing,
Come for to show you my diamond ring. (twice)

Dixie
Daniel D. Emmett

C
I wish I was in the land of cotton,
F
Old times there are not forgotten,
C   G7   C
Look away, look away, look away, Dixie Land!

F
In Dixie Land where I was born in
C   G7   C
Early on one frosty mornin',
C   G7   C
Look away, look away, look away, Dixie Land!

Chorus:
       F   D7   G7
Then I wish I was in Dixie, hooray! hooray!
C   F
In Dixie Land I'll take my stand
C   D7 G7 C   G7
To live and die in Dixie, away, away,
                           Dm
C
Away down south in Dixie, away, away,
A7   D7   G7 C
Away down south in Dixie.

Old Mrs. marry Will the Weaver,
William was a gay deceiver,
Look away, etc.
But when he put his arm around her,
He smiled as fierce as a forty-pounder,
Look away, etc.

His face was sharp as a butcher's cleaver,
But that did not seem to grieve her,
Look away, etc.
Old Mrs. acted the foolish part,
And died for a man that broke her heart,
Look away, etc.

Darlin' Corey

         A
Wake up, wake up, darlin' Corey,
What makes you sleep so sound?
The revenue officers are comin'
Gonna tear your still-house down.

Go 'way, go 'way darlin' Corey,
Quit hangin' around my bed,
Pretty women run me distracted,
Corn liquor's killed me most dead.

Oh yes, oh yes my darlin',
I'll do the best I can,
But I'll never give my pleasure,
To another gamblin' man.

The first time I saw darlin' Corey,
She was standing on the banks of the sea,
She had a pistol strapped around her body,
And a banjo on her knee.

The last time I saw darlin' Corey,
She had a dram glass in her hand,
She was drinkin' down her troubles,
With a low down gamblin' man.

Dig a hole, dig a hole in the meadow,
Dig a hole in the cold, cold ground,
Go and dig me a hole in the meadow,
Just to lay darlin' Corey down.

Don't you hear them blue-birds singing?
Don't you hear that mournful sound?
They're preachin' Corey's funeral,
In the lonesome graveyard ground.

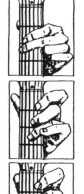

The Eyes Of Texas
Tune: *I've Been Working On The Railroad*

G
The eyes of Texas are upon you
C   G
All the livelong day.

The eyes of Texas are upon you.
A7   D7
You cannot get away.

Do not think you can escape them
C   B7
From night till early in the morn.
C   G
The eyes of Texas are upon you
D7
Till Gabriel blows his horn.

35

Buffalo Gals

C
As I was walking down the street,
G7   C
Down the street, down the street,

A pretty girl I chanced to meet,
    G   C
And we danced by the light of the moon.

Chorus:

F   C
Buffalo gal won't you come out tonight,
G7   C
Come out tonight, come out tonight?
F   C
Buffalo gal won't you come out tonight,
     G7   C
And dance by the light of the moon?

Old Joe Clark

Old Joe Clark had a house
Fifteen stories high,
And every story in that house
Was filled with chicken pie.

I went down to old Joe's house,
He invited me to supper,
I stumped my toe on the table leg
And stuck my nose in the butter.

Now I wouldn't marry a widder,
Tell you the reason why,
She'd have so many children
They'd make those biscuits fly.

Sixteen horses in my team,
The leaders they are blind,
And every time the sun goes down
There's a pretty girl on my mind.

Eighteen miles of mountain road
And fifteen miles of sand,
If I ever travel this road again,
I'll be a married man.

Old Joe Clark, the preacher's son,
Preached all over the plain,
The only text he ever knew
Was "High, low jack and the game."

Old Joe Clark had a mule,
His name was Morgan Brown,
And every tooth in that mule's head
Was sixteen inches around.

Old Joe Clark had a yellow cat,
She would neither sing or pray,
She stuck her head in the buttermilk jar
And washed her sins away.

Down In The Valley

D
Down in the valley, valley so low.
         A7   D
Hang your head over, hear the wind blow.
D
Hear the wind blow, dear, hear the wind blow.
          A7   D
Hang your head over, hear the wind blow.

Roses love sunshine, violets love dew
Angels in heaven, know I love you.
Know I love you dear, know I love you
Angels in heaven, know I love you.

If you don't love me, love whom you please
Throw your arms round me, give my heart ease.
Give my heart ease love, give my heart ease
Throw your arms round me, give my heart ease.

Build me a castle forty feet high
So I can see him as he rides by.
As he rides by love, as he rides by
So I can see him as he rides by.

Write me a letter, send it by mail
Send it in care of Birmingham jail.
Birmingham jail love, Birmingham jail
Send it in care of Birmingham jail.

36

Don't Let Your Deal Go Down

D   G
I've been all around this whole wide world
C   F
Way down in Memphis Tennessee.
D   D
Any old place I hang my hat
C   F
Seems like home to me.

Chorus:

D   G
Don't let your deal go down.
C   F
Don't let your deal go down.
D   G
Don't let your deal go down sweet mama
C   F
For my last old dollar's gone.

When I left my love behind,
She's standin' in the door,
She throwed her little arms around my neck and said,
"Sweet daddy please don't go."

Now it's who's gonna shoe your pretty little feet?
Who's gonna glove your hand?
And who's gonna kiss your ruby lips
Honey, who's gonna be your man?

She says, papa will shoe my pretty little feet,
Mama will glove my hand,
You can kiss my rosy lips
When you get back again.

Goodnight Ladies

A
Goodnight ladies,
      E7
Goodnight ladies,
A   D
Goodnight ladies,
    A   E7   A
We're going to leave you now.

Merrily we roll along,
E7   A
Roll along, roll along,

Merrily we roll along,
   E7   A
Over the deep blue sea.

Farewell ladies,
Farewell ladies,
Farewell ladies,
We're going to leave you now.

Sweet dreams, ladies,
Sweet dreams, ladies,
Sweet dreams, ladies,
We're going to leave you now.

The Foggy Dew

Bm   Em   A   Bm   Em   Bm
Over the hills I went one day, a lovely maid I spied.
           Em   A
With her coal black hair and her mantle so green,
      Bm   Em Bm
    an image to perceive.
    D   G   D   A
Says I, "Dear girl, will you be my bride
         Bm   Em F m Bm
    and she lifted her eyes of   blue;
               Em   A
She smiled and said, "Young man I'm to wed,
     Bm   Em   Bm
I'm to meet him in the foggy dew."

Over the hills I went one morn, a-singing I did go.
Met this lovely maid with her coal-black hair,
and she answered soft and low:
Said she, "Young man, I'll be your bride,
if I know that you'll be true."
Oh, in my arms, all her charms
were casted in the foggy dew.

Now the boss was a fine man down to the ground,
And he married a lady, six feet round,
She baked good bread, and she baked it well,
But she baked it as hard as the holes in hell.

37

Drill Ye Tarriers, Drill

Thomas F. Casey

Am
Early in the morning at seven o'clock
    E7
There are twenty tarriers a drilling at the 'rock,
    Am
And the boss comes around and he says "Keep still!
    E7
And come down heavy on your cast iron drill."

Chorus:
    Am   E7   Am
And drill ye tarriers, drill.
    G   Am
Drill ye tarriers drill.

Well you work all day for the sugar in your tay

Down behind the railway
    Am   E7   Am
And drill ye tarriers, drill,

And blast and fire.

Now our new foreman was Jim McGann,
By golly, he was, a blame mean man
Last week a premature blast went off,
And a mile in the sky went Big Jim Goff.

Now when next payday comes around,
Jim Goff a dollar short was found,
When asked the reason, came this reply,
"You were docked for the time you were up in the sky."

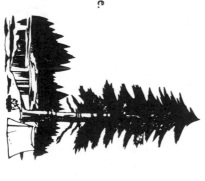

For He's A Jolly Good Fellow

F   BbF
For he's a jolly good fellow,
    C7   F
For he's a jolly good fellow,
                BbBdim
For he's a jolly good fellow,
    F   C7 F
Which nobody can deny!

We won't go home until morning, (3 times)
Till daylight doth appear!

The bear went over the mountain, (3 times)
To see what he could see!
(Yell) And all that he could see was

The other side of the mountain, (3 times)
Was all that he could see!

Corinna

E   A7
Corinna, Corinna

Where you been so long?   E
    B7
Corinna, Corinna
         E
Where you been so long?

Corinna, Corinna, why'd you leave me alone?
Corinna, Corinna, got no place to call my own.

Corinna, Corinna, bye-bye, so long,
Bye-bye, Corinna, bye-bye, so long.
Corinna, Corinna, bye-bye, so long,
I'll have the blues, Corinna, long as you stay gone.

Where did you get them high-heel shoes
And that dress you wear so fine?
Got my shoes from a railroad man
Dress from a driver in the mine.

Froggie Went A-Courtin'

D
Froggie went a-courtin' and he did ride, a-huh, a-huh,
         G   D
Froggie went a-courtin' and he did ride,
     A7   D
Sword and pistol by his side, a-huh, a-huh.

Well, he rode down to Miss Mouse's door, a-huh, a-huh,
Well, he rode down to Miss Mouse's door,
Where he had often been before, a-huh, a-huh.

He took Miss Mousie on his knee, a-huh, a-huh,
He took Miss Mousie on his knee,
Said, "Miss Mousie will you marry me?" A-huh, a-huh.

"I'll have to ask my Uncle Rat, etc.
See what he will say to that.", etc.

"Without my Uncle Rat's consent,
I would not marry the President."

Well, Uncle Rat laughed and shook his fat sides,
To think his niece would be a bride.

Well, Uncle Rat rode off to town
To buy his niece a wedding gown.

"Where will the wedding supper be?"
"Way down yonder in a hollow tree."

"What will the wedding supper be?"
"A fried mosquito and a roasted flea."

First to come in were two little ants,
Fixing around to have a dance.

Next to come in was a bumble bee,
Bouncing a fiddle on his knee.

Next to come in was a fat sassy lad,
Thinks himself as big as his dad.

Thinks himself a man indeed,
Because he chews the tobacco weed.

And next to come in was a big tomcat,
He swallowed the frog and the mouse and the rat.

Next to come in was a big old snake,
He chased the party into the lake.

Old MacDonald Had A Farm

F   Bb   F
Old MacDonald had a farm,
G   C   F
E - I, E - I, Oh!
                 Bb   F
And on this farm he had some chicks,
G7 C7 F
E - I, E - I, Oh!

With a chick chick here

And a chick chick there,
Bb
Here a chick, there a chick,
F   Gm
Everywhere a chick chick,
F   Bb   F
Old MacDonald had a farm,
G7 C7 F
E - I, E - I, Oh!

Ducks—quack, quack

Dogs—bow, wow

Cows—moo, moo

Pigs—oink, oink.

Etc.

The Strawberry Roan

C   G7
I was hangin' round town just a spendin' my time,

Out of a job and not makin' a dime,
                F   C
When a feller steps up and says, "I suppose

G7   C
You're a bronc rider, by the looks of your clothes."
                            G7
"You got me right, and a good one," I claim,
                      C   F
"Do you happen to have any bad ones to tame?"

He says: "I've got one and a bad one to buck,
      G7   F   C
And at throwin' good riders he's had lots of luck."

Chorus:

      G7   C
Well, it's Oh, that Strawberry Roan;
F   F   C
Oh, that Strawberry Roan.
            F   C
They say he's a cayuse that's never been rode,
        F   C
The man that gets on him is bound to be throwed,
      G7   C
Get off that Strawberry Roan.

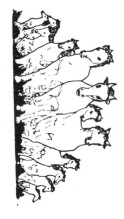

I gets all excited and I ask what he pays
To ride this old goat for a couple of days.
He offers a ten spot. I says, "I'm your man,
For the bronc never lived that I couldn't fan;
No, the bronc never lived, nor he never drew breath
That I couldn't ride till he starved plumb to death."
He says, "Get your saddle, I'll give you a chance."
We got in the buckboard and rode to the ranch.

Chorus:
Well, it's Oh, that strawberry roan,
Oh, that strawberry roan!
We stayed until morning, and right after chuck
We goes out to see how this outlaw can buck,
Oh, that strawberry roan!

Down in the horse corral standing alone
Is this old caballo, a strawberry roan.
His legs is all spavined, he has pigeon toes,
Two little pig eyes and a big Roman nose.
Little pin ears that touched at the tips,
And a big 44 run on his left hip.
He's ewe-necked and old, with a long lower jaw,
I could see with one eye he was a reg'lar outlaw.

Groundhog

E   D   E
Whet up your axe and whistle up your dog,
      A   B7
Whet up your axe and whistle up your dog,
E   B7   E   B7
We're off to the woods, to hunt ground hog,

Refrain:

E
Ground hog.
Old Joe Digger, Sam and Dave (twice)
Went a-hog hunting as hard as they could stave,
Groundhog.

Too many rocks, too many logs,
Too many rocks to hunt groundhogs.

He's in here, boys, the hole's wore slick,
Run here, Sam, with your forked stick.

Stand back, boys, let's be wise,
I think I see his beaded eyes.

Yonder comes Sam with a ten-foot pole,
To roust that groundhog out of his hole.

Grab him by the tail and pull him out,
Great God Almighty, ain't a groundhog stout?

Here he comes all in a whirl,
He's the biggest groundhog in this world.

Work, boys, work, hard as you can tear,
The meat'll do to eat and the hide'll do to tear.

Skin him out and tan his hide,
Best durn shoestrings ever I tried.

I love my groundhog stewed and fried,
Little plate of soup a-sittin' by the side.

The children screamed, the children cried,
They love that groundhog cooked and fried.

Up stepped Sal with a snigger and a grin,
Groundhog grease all over her chin.

Hello, Mamma, make Sam quit,
He's eatin' all the hog and don't leave me a bit.

Hello, boys, ain't it a sin,
Watch that gravy run down Sam's chin.

Watch him, boys, he's about to fall,
He's et 'til his pants won't button at all.

Hard, Ain't It Hard

D   G
First time I seen my true love
D   A7
He was walkin' by my door
     D
The last time I saw
     G
His false hearted smile
A7   D
Dead on his coolin' board.

Chorus:

                  G
It's hard and it's hard ain't it hard
     D   A7
To love one that never did love you
D   G
Hard and it's hard ain't it hard, great God,
    A7   D
To love one that never will be true.

There is a house in this old town,
That's where my true love lays around.
Takes other women right down on his knee
Tells them a tale that he won't tell me.

Don't go to drinkin' and to gamblin',
Don't go there your sorrows to drown.
This hard-liquor place is a low-down disgrace,
The meanest damn place in this town.

41

The Gray Goose

D
Well last Monday morning,
A
Lord, Lord, Lord,
Well last Monday morning,
D
Lord, Lord, Lord.

My daddy went a-huntin', Lord, Lord, Lord (twice)

Well along come a grey goose, Lord . . . etc.

Throwed the gun to his shoulder, etc.

Well, he pulled on the trigger, etc.

He was six weeks a-fallin', etc.

He was six weeks a-findin', etc.

And we put him on the wagon, etc.

And we took him to the farmhouse, etc.

He was six weeks a-pickin', etc.

And we put him on to parboil, etc.

He was six months a-parboil, etc.

And we put him on the table, etc.

Now the forks couldn't stick him, etc.

And the knife couldn't cut him, etc.

And we throwed him in the hogpen, etc.

And he broke the sow's jawbone, etc.

And we took him to the sawmill, etc.

And he broke the saw's teeth out, etc.

And the last time I seed him, etc.

He was flyin' 'cross the ocean, etc.

With a long string of goslin's, etc.

And he's goin', "Quank, quink-quank," etc.

Greensleeves

Em   D
A-las my love, you do me wrong,
C   B7
To cast me off discourteously;
Em   D
And I have lovéd you so long,
C   B7   Em
Delighting in your company.
G   D
Greensleeves was all my joy
Em   B7
Greensleeves was my delight,
G   D
Greensleeves was my heart of gold,
Em   B7   Em
And who but my lady Greensleeves.

I have been ready at your hand,
To grant whatever you would crave;
I have both wagered life and land,
Your love and good-will for to have.
If you intend thus to disdain,
It does the more enrapture me,
And even so, I still remain
A lover in captivity.

My men were clothed all in green,
And they did ever wait on thee;
All this was gallant to be seen;
And yet thou wouldst not love me.
Thou couldst desire no earthly thing
But still thou hadst it readily.
Thy music still to play and sing;
And yet thou wouldst not love me.

Well, I will pray to God on high,
That thou my constancy mayst see,
And that yet once before I die,
Thou wilt vouchsafe to love me.
Ah, Greensleeves, now farewell, adieu,
To God I pray to prosper thee,
For I am still thy lover true,
Come once again and love me.

Nine Pound Hammer

G
This nine-pound hammer is a little too heavy,
           C
Buddy, for my size, buddy for my size.
      D7   G

Chorus:

               C
So roll on, buddy, don't you roll so slow.
          D7   G
How can I roll, when the wheels won't go?

Ain't nobody's hammer in this mountain
That rings like mine, that rings like mine.

Well I went up on the mountain just to see my baby
And I ain't a-coming back, Lord,
   I ain't a-coming back.

It's a long way to Hazard, it's a long way to Harlan
Just to get a little booze, just to get a little booze.

Times Are Getting Hard

F   Gm7
Times are gettin' hard, boys,
C7   F
Money's gettin' scarce,
             G7
If times don't get no better, boys,
     C7   F
I'm bound to leave this place.
           Gm7
Take my true love by the hand,
C7   F
Lead her through the town,
F   Gm7
Say goodbye to everyone,
     C7   F
Goodbye to everyone.

Take my Bible from the bed,
Shotgun from the wall,
Take old Sal and hitch her up,
The wagon for to haul.
Pile the chairs and beds up high,
Let nothing drag the ground,
Sal can pull and we can push,
We're bound to leave this town.

Made a crop a year ago,
It withered to the ground,
Tried to get some credit
But the banker turned me down.
Goin' to Californi-ay,
Where everything is green,
Goin' to have the best old farm
That you have ever seen.

Oh, Susanna

     D   A7
I come from Alabama with a banjo on my knee,
          D   A7   D
I'm goin' to Lou'siana, my true love for to see.
     D   A7
It rained all night the day I left, the weather it was dry,
                 D   A7   D
The sun so hot I froze to death, Susanna don't you cry.

Chorus:

G   D   A7
Oh, Susanna, Oh, don't you cry for me.
          D   A7   D
I come from Alabama with a banjo on my knee.

I had a dream the other night,
When everything was still
I dreamed I saw Susanna
A-coming down the hill.

A red red rose was in her cheek,
A tear was in her eye
I said to her, Susanna girl,
Susanna don't you cry.

43

Tom Dooley

G
Hang down your head Tom Dooley,

Hang down your head and cry,
D
Killed poor Laura Foster,
G
You know you're bound to die.

You took her on the hillside
As God almighty knows,
You took her on the hillside
And there you hid her clothes.

You took her by the roadside
Where you begged to be excused,
You took her by the roadside
Where there you hid her shoes.

You took her on the hillside
To make her your wife,
You took her on the hillside
Where there you took her life.

Take down my old violin
And play it all you please,
At this time tomorrow
It'll be no use to me.

I dug a grave four feet long,
I dug it three feet deep,
And throwed the cold clay o'er her
And tramped it with my feet.

This world and one more then
Where do you reckon I'd be,
If it hadn't been for Grayson
I'd-a-been in Tennesse.

Rock Island Line

Chorus:

G
I say the Rock Island Line is a mighty good road,
G   A7   D7
I say the Rock Island Line is the road to ride
G
Oh, the Rock Island Line is a mighty good road,
C   C7
If you want to ride it, got to ride it like you find it,
G   D7   G
Buy your ticket at the station on the Rock Island Line.

Verses:

G
Jesus died to save our sins,
D
Glory be to God, gonna need him again.
A-B-C, Double X-Y-Z,
D7   G
Cat's in the cupboard but he can't see me.

I may be right and I may be wrong,
I know you're gonna miss me when I'm gone.

Red River Valley

E   B7   E
From this valley they say you are going,
E   E7   A   B7
We will miss your bright eyes and sweet smile;
E   E7   A   B7
For they say you are taking the sunshine
E   B7   E
That has brightened our pathways awhile.

Chorus:

E   B7   E
Come and sit by my side, if you love me,
E   B7
Do not hasten to bid me adieu,
E   E7   A
Just remember the Red River Valley
E   B7   E
And the cowboy who loved you so true.

I've been thinking a long time, my darling,
Of the sweet words you never would say,
Now, alas, must my fond hopes all vanish?
For they say you are going away.

Do you think of the valley you're leaving?
O how lonely and how dreary it will be.
Do you think of the kind hearts you're breaking?
And the pain you are causing to me?

They will bury me where you have wandered,
Near the hills where the daffodils grow,
When you're gone from the Red River Valley,
For I can't live without you I know.

Riddle Song

D
I gave my love a cherry that had no stone;
A7   D   A7
I gave my love a chicken that no bone;
         D   A7
I told my love a story that had no end;
D   G   D
I gave my love a baby that's no cryin'.

How can there be a cherry that has no stone?
How can there be a chicken that has no bone?
How can there be a story that has no end?
How can there be a baby that's no crying?

A cherry when it's blooming, it has no stone,
A chicken when it's pippin' it has no bone;
The story that I love you, it has no end,
A baby when it's sleeping, it's no crying.

Little Brown Jug

    A   D
My wife and I lived all alone,
   E7   A
In a little log hut we call'd our own.
          D
She loved gin and I loved rum,
 E7   A
I tell you we had lots of fun.
Chorus:
         D
Ha! Ha! Ha! you and me,
E7   A
Little brown jug don't I love thee!
         D
Ha! Ha! Ha! you and me,
E7   A
Little brown jug don't I love thee!

'Tis you who makes my friends and foes,
'Tis you who makes me wear old clothes,
Here you are so near my noes,
so tip her up and down she goes.
Chorus:

When I go toiling to my farm,
I take little brown jug under my arm,
Place him under a shady tree,
Little brown jug, 'tis you and me,
Chorus:

If I'd a cow that gave such milk,
I'd clothe her in the finest silk,
I'd feed her on the choicest hay,
And milk her forty times a day.
Chorus:

The rose is red, my nose is too,
The violets blue and so are you,
And yet I guess, before I stop
I'd better take another drop.
Chorus:

45

Midnight Special

G   C
Well you wake up in the morning,
         G
Hear the ding dong ring,
         D7
You go a-marching to the table,
        G
See the same damn thing;
        C
Well, it's on a one table,
        G
Knife, a fork and a pan,
         D7
And if you say anything about it,
          G
You're in trouble with the man.

Chorus:
       C
Let the midnight special
          G
Shine her light on me;
        D7
Let the midnight special
C   D7   G
Shine her ever loving light on me.

If you ever go to Houston,
You better walk right;
You better not stagger,
You better not fight;
Sheriff Benson will arrest you,
He'll carry you down,
And if the jury finds you guilty,
Penitentiary bound.

Mama Don't 'Low

     A
Mama don't 'low no banjo playin' round here.
                 E7
I say that mama don't 'low no banjo playin' round here.
   A   A7
Well, I don't care what mama don't 'low,
   D   Dm
Gonna play my banjo anyhow,
   A   E7   A
Mama don't 'low no banjo playin' here.

Mama don't 'low no guitar playin' round here.
Mama don't 'low no bass playin' round here, etc.
Mama don't 'low no talkin' round here, etc.
Gonna shoot my mouth off anyhow, etc.

Mama don't 'low no singin' round here, etc.,
Gonna sing my head off anyhow, etc.

Salty Dog Blues

Chorus:

F
Let me be your salty dog,
        D7
Let me be your salty dog,
     G7
Or I won't be your man at all,
C7   F
Honey, let me be your salty dog.

Verses:

F
Standing on the corner with the low-down blues,
     G7   D7
A great big hole in the bottom of my shoes,
C7   F
Honey, let me be your salty dog.

Look here, Sal, I know you,
With a low-down slipper and a brogan shoe,
Honey, let me be your salty dog.

We pulled the trigger and the gun said go,
The shot rung over in Mexico,
Honey, let me be your salty dog.

Yonder come little Rosie,
How in the world do you know,
I can tell her by her apron,
And the dress she wore.
Umbrella on her shoulder,
Piece of paper in her hand,
She goes a-marching to the captain,
Says I want my man.

46

Railroad Bill

Chorus:

D
Railroad Bill, Railroad Bill,
         G
He never worked and he never will
     D   A7   D
I'm gonna ride old Railroad Bill.

Verses:

D
Railroad Bill he was a mighty mean man
                                    G
He shot the midnight lantern out the brakeman's hand
    D   A7   D
I'm going to ride old Railroad Bill.

Railroad Bill took my wife,
Said if I didn't like it, he would take my life,
I'm going to ride old Railroad Bill.

Going up on a mountain, going out west,
Thirty-eight special sticking out of my vest,
I'm going to ride old Railroad Bill.

Buy me a pistol just as long as my arm,
Kill everybody ever done me harm,
I'm going to ride old Railroad Bill.

I've got a thirty-eight special on a forty-five frame,
How in the world can I miss him when I got dead aim,
I'm going to ride old Railroad Bill.

Polly Wolly Doodle

       G
Oh I went down South for to see my Sal,
                                    D7
Sing polly wolly doodle all the day,

My Sal she is a spunky gal,
                          G
Sing polly wolly doodle all the day.

Chorus:

G
Fare thee well, fare thee well,
                          D7
Fare thee well my fairy fay,

For I'm goin' to Lou'siana for to see my Susianna,
                                    G
Singing polly wolly doodle all the day.

Oh my Sal she is a maiden fair, etc.
With curly eyes and laughing hair, etc.

Things About Comin' My Way

        E
Ain't got no money,

Can't buy no grub,
                 A7
Back-bone and navel   E
Doing the belly rub.

Refrain:

E
Now after all my hard trav'ling,
                          B7   E
Things about comin' my way.

The pot was empty,
The cupboard bare
I said, "Mama,
What's going on here?"

The rent was due,
The light was out
I said, "Mama,
What's it all about?"

Sister was sick,
The doctor couldn't come
'Cause we couldn't pay him
The proper sum.

Old Blue

    C
Well, I had an old dog and his name was Blue;

          G7   C
I had an old dog and his name was Blue;

Well, I had an old dog and his name was Blue;

        G7   C
My old Blue was a good dog too.

Refrain:

           G7   C
Singin' ya old Blue, you good dog you.

Well, old Blue's feet was big and round (3 times)
He never 'lowed a possum to touch ground.

I'll take my axe and I'll take my horn
And I'll get me a possum in the new round courn.
Well old Blue barked and I went to see
And Blue had a possum up in a tree.

Well the possum crawled out on a limb
Blue barked at the possum, possum growled at him.
Well he treed a possum in a hollow log
You could tell from that he was a good old dog.

Well Blue, what makes your eyes so red (3 times)
You run that possum 'til you're almost dead.

Well when old Blue died he died so hard
He shook the ground in my back yard
I dug his grave with a silver spade
And lowered him down with a golden chain.

Now every time I hear Blue bark (3 times)
He's treeing possums in Noah's ark

Well I'm gonna tell you so you know (3 times)
That old Blue's gone where the good dogs go.

Well there's only one thing that troubles my mind
Blue's gone to heaven left me behind.

48

Loch Lomond

Lady Scott

       G   C
By yon bonnie banks and by yon bonnie braes,

D7   G   C   G7   C G
Where the sun shines bright on Loch Lomond,

          Em   G   C
Where me and my true love were ever wont to go,

D7   G   C   G   D7G
On the bonnie, bonnie banks of Loch Lomond.

Chorus:

D7   G   B7   EmC   G D7
Oh, you'll take the high road and I'll take the low road,

     EmC   G   C   G
And I'll be in Scotland afore ye,

     Em   G   C
But me and my true love will never meet again

D7   G   C   G   D7G
On the bonnie, bonnie banks of Loch Lomond.

'Twas then that we parted in yon shady glen,
On the steep, steep side of Ben Lomond,
Where in purple hue the Highland hills we view
And the moon coming out in the gloaming.

The wee birdies sing and the wild flowers spring,
And in sunshine the waters are sleeping,
But the broken heart it kens nae second spring again
Though the woeful may cease from their greeting.

St. James Infirmary

<pre>
      Am   E7   Am
It was down in old Joe's barroom.
      Dm   G7   C   E7
On the corner by the square,
      Am   E7   Am
The drinks were served as usual
        E7   Am
And the usual crowd was there.
</pre>

Now on my left stood big Joe McKennedy,
And his eyes were bloodshot red,
And he looked at the gang aroúnd him,
And these were the very words he said.

I went down to the St. James Infirmary,
I saw my baby there,
She was stretched out on a long, white table,
So cold, so pale, and fair.

Let her go, let her go, God bless her,
Wherever she may be.
She can ramble this wide world over,
And never find another man like me.

Now when I die please bury me,
In my hightop Stetson hat,
Just put a twenty dollar gold piece on my watch chain,
So the gang will know I'm standing pat.

I want six crap shooters for my pall bearers,
And a chorus girl to sing me a song,
Put a jazz band on my hearse wagon,
Just to raise hell as we roll along.

And now that you have heard my story,
I'll take another shot of booze,
If anyone should happen to ask you,
Well, I've got the gambler's blues.

I've Been Workin' On The Railroad

<pre>
G   C   G
I've been workin' on the railroad, all the live-long day;

I've been workin' on the railroad,
    A7   D7
just to pass the time away.
                         G
Don't you hear the whistle blowin,
C   B7
rise up so early in the morn,
C   G
Don't you hear the captain shoutin':
    D7   G
 "Dinah, blow your horn."

G   C
Dinah, won't you blow, Dinah won't you blow,
    D7   G
Dinah won't you blow your horn.
G   C
Dinah, won't you blow, Dinah won't you blow,
    D7
Dinah won't you blow your horn.

                                    C
Someone's in the kitchen with Dinah;
                      D7
someone's in the kitchen I know
G   C
Someone's in the kitchen with·Dinah,
    D7   G
strummin' on the old banjo.

Fee, fie, fiddle-i-o, fee, fie fiddle-i-o-o,
Fee, fie, fiddle-i-o, strummin' on the old banjo.
</pre>

Someone's makin' love to Dinah,
someone's makin' love I know,
Someone's makin' love to Dinah,
'cause I can't hear the old banjo.

No one's in the kitchen with Dinah,
no one's in the kitchen I know,
No one's in the kitchen with Dinah,
'cause Dinah's got B.O.

This Train

E
This train is bound for glory, this train,
E   E7
This train is bound for glory,
E   E7
This train is bound for glory,
A
Don't ride nothin' but the righteous and the holy,
          B7   E
This train is bound for glory, this train.

This train don't carry no gamblers, this train,
This train don't carry no gamblers, this train.
This train don't carry no gamblers,
No hypocrites, no midnight ramblers,
This train is bound for glory, this train.

This train is built for speed now, etc.
Fastest train you ever did see,
This train is bound for glory, this train.

This train don't carry no liars, etc.
No hypocrites and no high flyers,
This train is bound for glory, this train.

This train you don't pay no transportation, etc.
No Jim Crow and no discrimination,
This train is bound for glory, this train.

This train don't carry no rustlers, etc.
Sidestreet walkers, two-bit hustlers,
This train is bound for glory, this train.

On Top Of Old Smoky

C   F
On top of old Smoky
C
All covered with snow,
          G7
I lost my true lover,
          C
From courting too slow

          F
Now courting is pleasure
          C
And parting is grief,
             G7
And a false hearted lover,
          C
Is worse than a thief.

Say a thief will just rob you
And take what you have
But a false hearted lover
Will lead you to the grave.

And the grave will decay you
And turn you to dust
Not one boy in a hundred
A poor girl can trust.

They'll hug you and kiss you
And tell you more lies
Than the cross-ties on the railroad
Or the stars in the skies.

So come all you young maidens
And listen to me
Never place your affection
On a green willow tree.

For the leaves they will wither
And the roots they will die
You'll all be forsaken
And never know why.
On top of Old Smoky
All covered with snow
I lost my true lover
From courting too slow.

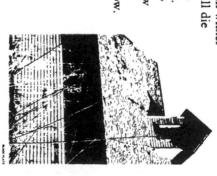

Three Blind Mice

D   A7   D
Three blind mice, three blind mice,
A7   D   A7   D
See how they run, see how they run;
      A7   D
They all ran after the farmer's wife,
          A7   D
She cut off their tails with a carving knife,
          A7   D   A7
Did ever you see such a sight in your life,
D   A7   D
As three blind mice?

Molly Malone

C   Am   Dm   G7
In Dublin's fair city where the girls are so pretty,

C   Am   Dm   G7
'Twas there that I first met sweet Molly Malone.

C   Am
She wheeled her wheelbarrow

Dm   G7
through the streets broad and narrow,

C   Am   G7   C
Cryin' "Cockles and Mussels alive, alive-o!"

Chorus:

C   Am Dm   G7
Alive, alive-o,   alive, alive-o,

C   Am   G7   C
Crying "Cockles and Mussels alive, alive-o!"

She was a fishmonger, but sure 'twas no wonder,
For so were her father and mother before,
And they each pushed their wheelbarrow
through streets broad and narrow
Crying cockles and mussels alive, alive, oh!

She died of a "faver," and no one could save her,
And that was the end of sweet Molly Malone,
Her ghost wheels her barrow
through streets broad and narrow
Crying cockles and mussels alive, alive, oh!

Oh, Babe, It Ain't No Lie
Elizabeth Cotton

C
One old woman, Lord, in this town

           F
Keeps a-telling lies on me.

        C   G7   C
Wish to my soul that she would die, Lord,

C   F
She's telling lies on me.

Chorus:

C   F#dim G7   C
Oh, babe, it ain't no lie.

E7   F
Oh, babe, it ain't no lie.

           C
Oh, babe, it ain't no lie,

         G7   C
This life I'm livin' is very hard.

Been all around this whole round world,
Lord, and I just got back today.
Work all the week, honey and I give it all to you,
Honey baby, what more can I do?

Sally In Our Alley
Henry Carey

Bb   Cm7 Bb Cm Bb
Of all the girls that are so smart,

      Eb   F7   Bb
There's none like pretty Sally;

       Cm7 Bb Cm Bb
She is the darling of my heart,

      Eb   F7   Bb
And lives in our alley;

        Bb   Bb7 Eb
There's ne'er a lady in the land

G7 Cm G7 Cm C7 F
Is half so sweet as Sally;

F7   Gm Cm   Bb
She is the darling of my heart,

      Eb Cm F7 Bb
And lives in our alley.

Of all the days within the week
I dearly love but one day,
And that's the day that comes betwixt
A Saturday and Monday:
O, then I'm dressed all in my best
To walk a-broad with Sally;
She is the darling of my heart,
And lives in our alley.

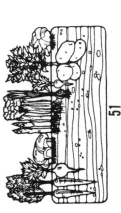

Devilish Mary

D
I once dressed up and went to town
Bn
To court a fair young lady.
D
I inquired about her name,
A7   D
Her name was Devilish Mary.

Chorus:

Bn
Come a-fa-la-ling,
A7 D
Come a-ling, come l'-ling,
D
Come a-fa-la-ling,
A7 D   A7 D
Come a dairy, come a dairy.

Me and Mary began to spark
She got all in a hurry,
I hadn't said but a single word
She'd marry the very next Thursday.

We had not been married for about two weeks
Before we ought to been parted;
She made it up all in her mind
She kicked up her heels and started.

She washed my clothes in old soap suds
She filled my bath with switches
She let me know right at the start
She was going to wear my britches.

He Was A Friend Of Mine

G7   C
He was a friend of mine
G7   C
He was a friend of mine.
F   C   E7   F
Never had no money to pay his fine
G7   C
He was a friend of mine.

He never done no wrong, (twice)
He was just a poor boy, a long way from home,
He was a friend of mine.

I stole away and cried, (twice)
Never had no money and I can't be satisfied,
He was a friend of mine.

He was a friend of mine, (twice)
When I hear his name
You know I just can't keep from crying,
He was a friend of mine.

He died on the road, (twice)
Never had no money (to) pay for his board,
He was a friend of mine.

The Dreary Black Hills

E
Kind friends, won't you listen to my pitiful tale,
B7
I'm an object of pity and looking quite stale,
A   E   B7   E
I gave up my job selling Aire's Patent Pills
A   E   B7   E
To prospect for gold in the Dreary Black Hills.

Chorus:

E
Don't travel away, stay at home if you can,
B7
Stay away from that city, they call it Cheyenne,
A   E   B7   E
Where the blue waters roll and Comanche Bill
A   E   B7   E
Will lift up your hair in the Dreary Black Hills.

The round house in Cheyenne is filled every night
With loafers and bummers of most every plight;
On their backs there's no clothes, in their pockets no bills,
Each night they keep leaving for the Dreary Black Hills.

I got to Cheyenne, no gold could I find,
And I thought of the maiden I'd left far behind;
The rain, hail and snow froze plumb to the gills,
They call me the orphan of the dreary Black Hills.

Kind friends, to conclude my advice I'll unfold,
Don't go to the Black Hills and search there for gold;
Railroad speculators their pockets you'll fill
By taking a trip to the Dreary Black Hills.

Now if I ever marry again
It'll be for love not riches,
Marry a little girl 'bout two feet high
So she can't wear my britches.

52

My Old Kentucky Home
Stephen Foster

```
D              D7      G          D
The sun shines bright on my old Kentucky home,
   Bm      E7     A    A7
Tis summer, the folks there are gay.
D           D7      G           D
The corn top's ripe and the meadow's in the bloom,
E7    D    A7    D
While the birds make music all the day.
D           D7   G       D
The young folks roll on the little cabin floor,
   Bm     E7    A    A7
All merry, all happy and bright.
     D        D7   G              D
By 'n by hard times comes a-knocking at the door,
E7     D     A7       D
Then my old Kentucky home, good night.
```

Chorus:
```
D     G      D
Weep no more, my lady,
F#7G      D
Oh, weep no more today.
   A7 D      D7      G
We will sing one song for the old Kentucky home,
E7    D     A7    D
For the old Kentucky home far away.
```

Pick A Bale Of Cotton

Chorus:
```
E              A            E
Oh, Lordy, pick a bale of cotton,
                    B7      E
Oh, Lordy, pick a bale a day.
E              A            E
Oh, Lordy, pick a bale of cotton.
                    B7      E
Oh, Lordy, pick a bale a day.
```

Verses:
```
E
Gonna jump down turn around,
     A           E
pick a bale of cotton,
Gonna jump down turn around,
   B7       E
pick a bale a day.
Gonna jump down turn around,
     A           E
pick a bale of cotton,
Gonna jump down turn around,
   B7       E
pick a bale a day.
```

```
E
Gonna get on my knees,
pick a bale of cotton,
Gonna get on my knees,
pick a bale a day.
Gonna get on my knees,
pick a bale of cotton,
Gonna get on my knees,
pick a bale a day.
```

Gonna jump, jump, jump down, etc.

Me and my gal gonna, etc.

Me and my buddy gonna, etc.

Gonna pick-a, pick-a, pick-a, pick-a, etc.

53

The Devil and The Farmer's Wife

Child Ballad 278

E
There was an old man lived over the hill,
A   B7
If he ain't moved away he's living there still
E
Singing fah-de-ing, ding

E
Dah-de-ing-ding

Di-di-um da-de ing ding

Didium da de ing ding
B7   E
Di-di-um day.

Well, the devil came up to him one day,
Said one of your family I'm gonna take away.
Singing etc.

Oh please don't take my eldest son,
There's work on the farm that's gotta be done.
Singing etc.

It's all I want, that wife of yours,
Well you can take her with all of my heart.
Singing etc.

Well, he picks the wife up upon his back,
And off to hell he goes clickity-clack.
Singing etc.

He carries her on about a mile down the road,
He said old woman you're a devil of a load.
Singing etc.

He carries her down to the gates of hell,
He says poke up the fire we'll scorch her well.
Singing etc.

There were two little devils with ball and with chain,
She ups with her foot and she kicks out their brains.
Singing etc.

And nine little devils went climbing up the wall,
Saying take her back daddy, she'll murder us all.
Singing etc.

He said here is your wife, both sound and well,
If I'd a kept her there longer she'd a torn up hell.
Singing etc.

Well, I got up next morning, I spied through a crack
I seen the old devil come a dragging her back.
Singing etc.

He said I've been a devil most all of my life,
But I'd never been in hell till I met with your wife.
Singing etc.

Now, this only goes to show, what a woman can do,
She can whup out the devil and her husband too.
Singing etc.

This shows that the women are better than men,
They can go down to hell and come back again.
Singing etc.

54

Little Maggie

D   C
Well yonder stands little Maggie,
D   C   D
With a dram glass in her hand,
    C
And she's drinkin' down her troubles,
D   C   D
And she's foolin' some other man.

Tell me how can I ever stand it,
Just to see those two blue eyes.
They're shining like a diamond,
Like a diamond in the sky.

Sometimes I have a nickel,
Sometimes I have a dime.
And it's sometimes I have ten dollars,
Just to buy Little Maggie some wine.

Now she's marching down to the station,
Got a suitcase in her hand.
She's going for to leave me,
She is bound for some distant land.

Pretty flowers were made for blooming,
Pretty stars were meant to shine.
Pretty girls were made for boys to love,
And Little Maggie was made for mine.

Well the first time I seen Little Maggie,
She was sitting by the banks of the sea.
Had a forty-five strapped around her shoulder,
And a banjo on her knee.

Old Dog Tray
Stephen Foster

    G   D7
The morn of life is past,
               G
And evening comes at last,
       D7   G   D7
It brings me a dream of a once happy day,
 G   D7
Of merry forms I've seen
            G
Upon the village green,
Am   G D7 G
Sporting with my old dog Tray.

Chorus:

D7   G
Old dog Tray's ever faithful,
D7   G
Grief cannot drive him away,
         D7
He's gentle, he is kind,
       G
I'll never never find
G7 C   G D7 G
A better friend than old dog Tray.

The forms I called my own
Have vanished one by one,
The loved ones, the dear ones,
Have all passed away.
Their happy smiles have flown,
Their gentle voices gone,
I've nothing left but old dog Tray.

Listen To The Mockingbird
Alice Hawthorne

F
Listen to the mockingbird,
            C7   F
I'm dreaming now of Hallie,
            C7   F
Sweet Hallie, sweet Hallie,
            C7   F
I'm dreaming now of Hallie,
F7   Bb   C7   F
For the thought of her is one that never dies.
         C7   F
She's sleeping in the valley,
       C7 F
The valley, the valley,
        C7   F
She's sleeping in the valley,
F7   Bb   C7   F
And the mockingbird is singing where she lies.

When thoughts recall the past,
His eyes are on me cast;
I know that he feels what my breaking heart would say.
Although he cannot speak,
I'll vainly, vainly seek
A better friend than old dog Tray.

Chorus:

F   C7
Listen to the mockingbird,
               F
Listen to the mockingbird,
       C   C7   F
The mockingbird is singing o'er her grave;
              C7
Listen to the mockingbird,
               F
Listen to the mockingbird,
D Gmin   C7   F
Still singing where the weeping willows wave.

Ah well I yet can remember, I remember, I remember
Ah well I yet can remember
When we gathered in the cotton side by side
'Twas in the mild mid-September, in September, in September
Twas in the mild mid-September
And the mocking bird was singing far and wide

When charms of spring are awaken, are awaken, are awaken, are awaken
When charms of spring are awaken
And the mocking bird is singing on the bough
I feel like one so forsaken, so forsaken, so forsaken
I feel like one so forsaken
Since my Hallie is no longer with me now

55

Hallelujah, I'm A Bum

F
Why don't you work like other men do?

C7
How the hell can I work when there's no work to do?

Chorus:

F
Hallelujah, I'm a bum

C7
Hallelujah, bum again!

F
Hallelujah, give us a handout

C7   F
To revive us again.

Oh, I love my boss, and my boss loves me,
And that is the reason that I'm so hungry.

Oh, springtime has come, and I'm just out of jail,
Without any money, and without any bail.

I went to a house, and I knocked on the door,
The lady said, "Run, bum, you've been here before."

I went to a house, and I asked for some bread;
A lady came out, said, "The baker is dead."

When springtime does come, oh, won't we have fun,
We'll throw up our jobs and we'll go on the bum.

If I was to work, and save all I earn,
I could buy me a bar and have money to burn.

I passed by a saloon, and heard someone snore,
And I found the bartender asleep on the floor.

I stayed there and drank till a copper came in,
And he put me asleep with a slap on the chin.

Next morning in court I was still in a haze
When the judge looked at me, he said, "Thirty days."

Stewball

E
Stewball was a good horse,

A
And he held a high head,

B7   E
And the mane on his fore-top

E
Was fine as silk thread.

I rode him in England,
I rode him in Spain,
And I never did lose boys,
I always did gain.

So come all of you gamblers,
From near and from far,
Don't bet your gold dollar
On that little gray mare.

As they were riding
'Bout half way 'round,
That gray mare she stumbled
And fell to the ground.

And away out yonder,
Ahead of them all,
Come dancing and prancing
My noble Stewball.

Stewball was a good horse,
And he held a high head,
And the mane on his foretop
Was fine as silk thread.

I rode him in England,
And I rode him in Spain,
And I never did lose boys,
I always did gain.

Most likely she'll stumble,
Most likely she'll fall,
But you never will lose
On my noble Stewball.

Sit tight in your saddle,
Let slack on your rein,
And you never will lose boys,
You always will gain.

Bowling Green

A   F#m
Wish I was in Bowling Green sittin' in a chair
A
One arm 'round my pretty little miss

                        F#m
the other 'round my dear

The other 'round my dear, Bowling Green
A F#m   A
Hey, good old Bowling Green.

If you see that man of mine, tell him once for me
If he loves another girl, yes I'll set him free . . .
Yes I'll set him free, Bowling Green
Hey, good old Bowling Green.

Wish I was a bumblebee sailing through the air
Sail right down to my feller's side, touch him if you dare.
Touch him if you dare, Bowling Green
Hey, good old Bowling Green.

Goin' through this whole wide world,
   I'm goin' through alone
Goin' through this whole wide world,
   I ain't got no home
I ain't got no home, Bowling Green
Hey, good old Bowling Green.

Sweet Evelina

     Bb
Way down in the meadow where the lily first blows,
            F7   Bb
Where the wind from the mountains ne'er ruffles the rose
                             Eb Bb
Lives fond Evelina, the sweet little dove,
    F7   Bb
The pride of the valley the girl that I love.

Chorus:

Bb
Dear Evelina, Sweet Evelina,
F7   Bb
My love for thee shall never die

Dear Evelina, Sweet Evelina,   Bb
F7
My love for thee shall never, never die.

She's fair like a rose, like a lamb she is meek,
And she never was known to put paint on her cheek;
In the most graceful curls hangs her raven black hair,
And she never requires perfumery there.

Evelina and I one fine evening in June
Took a walk all alone by the light of the moon;
The planets all shone for the heavens were clear,
And I felt round the heart tremendously queer.

Three years have gone by and I've not got a dollar,
Evelina still lives in that green grassy holler;
Although I am fated to marry her never,
I've sworn that I'll love her forever and ever.

On The Banks Of The Wabash

Paul Dresser

```
        G      C                    G  D7
'Round my Indiana homestead wave the cornfields,
  G     G7     A7    D7     G
In the distance loom the woodlands clear and cool,
       C             G  D7
Oftentimes my thoughts revert to scenes of childhood,
  G    G7     A7   D7    G
Where I first received my lessons, nature's school,
   B7                              Em
But one thing there is missing in the picture,
  A7                      D7
Without her face it seems so incomplete.
   G      C     G    D7
I long to see my mother in the doorway,
  G      G7   A7   D7   G
As she stood there years ago, her boy to greet.
```

Chorus:

```
    G                 B7             C
Oh, the moonlight's fair tonight along the Wabash,
E7            Am            D7
From the fields there comes the breath of new-mown hay.
         G             B7           C
Through the sycamores, the candle lights are gleaming,
C#dim  G     A7    D7 G
On the banks of the Wabash, far away.
```

The Colorado Trail

```
D              A7      A7      D
Eyes like the morning star,
A          D
Cheeks like a rose,
E             A             A
Concerning the great speckled bird,
A       A7      D
Remember his name is recorded,
       E                          A
In the great Book of God's Holy Word.

Annie was a pretty girl,
Bm                A7
God almighty knows.
D
Weep all you little rains,
A7          D
Wail winds wail,
Bm
All along, along, along
G            D
The Colorado Trail.
```

The Great Speckled Bird

```
A         A7        D
What a beautiful thought I'm thinking,
E                       A
Concerning the great speckled bird,
A       A7      D
Remember his name is recorded,
       E                          A
In the great Book of God's Holy Word.

The great speckled bird sits in splendor,
All surrounded and despised by the squab,
The great speckled bird is the Bible,
Representing the Great Church of God.

I am glad that I come to your meeting,
I'm proud that my name is of a bird,
For I want to be one never fearing,
In the arms of my Savior's true word.

When He comes, if He comes, I will greet Him,
On a cloud that is floating in the Word,
I will rise up my savior to greet Him,
On the wings of a great speckled bird.
```

Many years have passed since I strolled by the river,
Arm in arm with Sweetheart Mary by my side.
It was there I tried to tell her that I loved her,
It was there I begged of her to be my bride,
Long years have passed
  since I strolled through the church-yard,
She's sleeping there, my angel Mary dear.
I loved her but she thought I didn't mean it,
Still I'd give my future were she only there.

Jeanie With The Light Brown Hair
Stephen Foster

F
I dream of Jeanie with the light brown hair,
Dm   FBb   F   G7   C7
Borne, like a vapor, on the summer's air;
F
I see her tripping where the bright streams play,
G7   C   Dm   C   G7   C
Happy as the daisies that dance on her way.
C7   F
Many were the wild notes her merry voice would pour,
Bb   F   F7 Am   C7
Many were the blithe birds that warbled them o'er;
F
Ah! I dream of Jeanie with the light brown hair,
Gm6Dm Bb   F   Ab   G   C7   F
Floating   like a vapor on the soft summer air.

I long for Jeanie with the day-dawn smile,
Radiant in gladness, warm with winning guile;
I hear her melodies, like joys gone by,
Sighing round my heart o'er the fond hopes that die;
Sighing like the night wind and sobbing like the rain,
Waiting for the lost one that comes not again;
Ah! I long for Jeanie and my heart bows low,
Never more to find her where the bright waters flow.

Old Rattler

C
Rattler was a good old dog,
                    G7
As blind as he could be.

But every night at suppertime,
                    C
I believe that dog could see.

Chorus:
C
Here, Rattler, here,
              G7
Here, Rattler, here,

Call old Rattler from the barn,
                          C
Here, Rattler, here.

Rattler barked the other night,
I thought he treed a coon,
When I come to find him,
He's barkin' at the moon.

Rattler was a friendly dog,
Even though he was blind.
He wouldn't hurt a living thing,
He was so very kind.

One night I saw a big fat coon,
Climb into a tree.
I called Ol' Rattler right away,
To fetch him down for me.

But Rattler wouldn't fetch for me,
Because he liked that coon.
I saw them walkin' paw in paw,
Later by the light of the moon.

Grandpa had a muley cow,
Muley since she was born,
It took a jaybird forty years,
To fly from horn to horn.

Now old Rattler's dead and gone,
Like all the good dogs do.
Don't put on the dog yourself,
Or you'll be goin' there too.

Sometimes I Feel Like A Motherless Child

      Em
Sometimes I feel like a motherless child,
              Em
Sometimes I feel like a motherless child,
      Am
Sometimes I feel like a motherless child,
   Am Em   B7
A long way from home—
Em C B7   Em
A long way from home.

Sometimes I feel like I'm almost gone (3 times)
A long ways from home. (twice)

Sometimes I feel like a feather in the air (3 times)
A long ways from home. (twice)

59

The Foggy, Foggy Dew

When I was a bachelor, I lived all alone, [G] [C]
I worked at the weaver's trade; [D7] [G]
And the only only thing I did that was wrong [C]
Was to woo a fair young maid. [D7] [G]
I wooed her in the wintertime, [D7] [G]
Part of the summer too; [D7] [G]
And the only only thing I did that was wrong [C]
Was to keep her from the foggy, foggy dew. [D7] [G]

One night she knelt close by my side,
When I was fast asleep.
She threw her arms around my neck,
And then began to weep.
She wept, she cried, she tore her hair—
Ah me, what could I do?
So all night long I held her in my arms,
Just to keep her from the foggy, foggy dew.

Again I am a bachelor, I live with my son,
We work at the weaver's trade;
And every single time I look into his eyes
He reminds me of the fair young maid.
He reminds me of the wintertime
And of the summer too;
And the many, many times that I held her in my arms,
Just to keep her from the foggy, foggy dew.

Skip To My Lou

Lost my partner what'll I do, [D]
Lost my partner what'll I do, [A7]
Lost my partner what'll I do, [D]
Skip to my Lou my darling. [A7] [D]

Chorus:

Gone again, skip to my Lou, [D]
Gone again, skip to my Lou, [A7]
Gone again, skip to my Lou, [D]
Skip to my Lou my darling. [A7] [D]

I'll get another one prettier than you (3 times)
Skip to my Lou my darling.

Little red wagon painted blue, etc.

Flies in the buttermilk two by two, etc.

Flies in the sugar bowl shoo shoo shoo, etc.

Going to Texas two by two, etc.

Cat's in the cream jar what'll I do?, etc.

Gee, But I Want To Go Home

The coffee that they give us, [G]
They say is mighty fine, [D7] [G]
It's good for cuts and bruises [G]
And tastes like iodine.

Chorus:

I don't want no more of army life, [C]
Gee, but I want to go, Gee, but I want to go home. [D7] [G] [D7] [G]

The biscuits that they give us,
They say are mighty fine,
One fell off a table
And killed a pal of mine.

The clothes that they give us,
They say are mighty fine,
Me and my buddy,
Can both fit into mine.

They treat us all like monkeys
And make us stand in line,
They give you fifty dollars a week
And take back forty-nine.

The girls at the service club
They say are mighty fine,
Most are over eighty
And the rest are under nine.

The Titanic

D   G   D
Oh they built the ship Titanic to sail the ocean blue,

And they thought they had a ship
        E7   A7
that the water would never go thru,
     D
But the Lord's Almighty hand
                G   D
knew that ship would never land,
         A7   D
It was sad when that great ship went down.

Chorus:

    G   D
It was sad—It was sad.
                           A7
It was sad when the great ship went down.
     (To the bottom of the)
D   D7   G
Husbands and wives, little children lost their lives—
  D   A7   D
It was sad when that great ship went down.

Oh, they sailed from England,
   and were almost to the shore,
When the rich refused to associate with the poor,
So they put them down below,
  where they were the first to go,
It was sad when the great ship went down.

The boat was full of sin, and the sides about to burst,
When the captain shouted, "A-women and children first!"
Oh, the captain tried to wire, but the lines were all on fire,
It was sad when the great ship went down.

Worried Man Blues

G
It takes a worried man to sing a worried song.
                                      G
It takes a worried man to sing a worried song.
 C
It takes a worried man to sing a worried song.
                       G
         D7
I'm worried now but I won't be worried long.

I went across the river, and I lay down to sleep (3 times)
When I woke up, had shackles on my feet.

Twenty nine links of chain around my leg (3 times)
And on each link, an initial of my name.

I asked that judge, tell me, what's gonna be my fine
   (3 times)
Twenty-one years on the Rocky Mountain line.

The train arrived, sixteen coaches long (3 times)
The girl I love, she's on that train and gone.

I looked down the track, as far as I could see (3 times)
A little bitty hand, was waving after me.

If anyone should ask you, who made up this song
   (3 times)
Tell 'em it was me, and I sing it all day long.

Oh, they swung the lifeboats out
   o'er the deep and ragin' sea,
When the band struck up with,
   "A-nearer My God to Thee."
Little children wept and cried,
   as the waves swept o'er the side,
   It was sad when the great ship went down.

Sally Goodin

E
Had a piece of pie an' I had a piece of puddin',
                    C#m
An' I gave it all away just to see my Sally Goodin.
E
Had a piece of pie an' I had a piece of puddin',
                    C#m
An' I gave it all away just to see my Sally Goodin.

E
Well, I looked down the road an' I see my Sally comin',
E   B7   E
An' I thought to my soul that I'd kill myself a-runnin'.
                  C#m
Well, I looked down the road an' I see my Sally comin',
        B7   E
An' I thought to my soul that I'd kill myself a-runnin'.

Love a 'tater pie an' I love an apple puddin',
An' I love a little gal that they call Sally Goodin.
Love a 'tater pie an' I love an apple puddin',
An' I love a little gal that they call Sally Goodin.
An' I dropped the 'tater pie an' I left the apple puddin',
But I went across the mountain to see my Sally Goodin.
An' I dropped the 'tater pie an' I left the apple puddin',
But I went across the mountain to see my Sally Goodin.

Sally is my dooxy an' Sally is my daisy,
When Sally says she hates me I think I'm goin' crazy.
Sally is my dooxy an' Sally is my daisy,
When Sally says she hates me I think I'm goin' crazy.
Little dog'll bark an' the big dog'll bite you,
Little gal'll court you an' big gal'll fight you.
Little dog'll bark an' the big dog'll bite you,
Little gal'll court you an' big gal'll fight you.

She'll Be Coming 'Round The Mountain

F
She'll be comin' 'round the mountain when she comes,
                   C7
She'll be comin' 'round the mountain when she comes,
F   F7
She'll be comin' 'round the mountain,
            Bb
She'll be comin' 'round the mountain,
F   C7   F
She'll be drivin' six white horses when she comes, etc.
She'll be shinin' just like silver when she comes, etc.
Oh, we'll all go out to meet her when she comes, etc.
She'll be breathin' smoke an' fire when she comes, etc.
We'll be singin' "hallelujah" when she comes, etc.
We will kill the old red rooster when she comes, etc.
We'll all have chicken an' some dumplin's
    when she comes, etc.

Rainin' an' a-pourin' an' the creek's runnin' muddy,
An' I'm so drunk, Lord, I can't stand studdy,
Rainin' an' a-pourin' an' the creek's runnin' muddy,
An' I'm so drunk, Lord, I can't stand studdy,
I'm goin' up the mountain an' marry little Sally,
Raise corn on the hillside an' the devil in the valley.
I'm goin' up the mountain an' marry little Sally,
Raise corn on the hillside an' the devil in the valley.

The Star Spangled Banner

Francis Scott Key/Tune: To Anacreon In Heaven

Ab   Fm C7 Fm   Bb 7 Eb
Oh say, can you see, by the dawn's early light,
      Ab Eb
What so proudly we hailed,
Eb7 Ab
at the twilight's last gleaming?
            Fm
Whose broad stripes and bright stars,
C7   Fm Bb7 Eb
thru the perilous fight,
      Ab   Eb
O'er the ramparts we watched,
Eb7 A   Eb 7
were so gallantly streaming?

And the rockets' red glare, the bombs bursting in air,
  Ab   Eb E7 Ab Ab Bb7 Eb
Gave proof thru the night, that our flag was still there,
Ab Bbm7 Ab Db F7 Bb7   Ab
Oh, say, does   that Star Spangled Banner yet wave,
Eb   Ab   Fm Bb7 Ab Eb7 Ab
O'er the land of the free and the home of the brave.

On the shore, dimly seen thro' the mists of the deep,
Where the foe's haughty host in dread silence reposes,
What is that which the breeze, o'er the towering steep,
As it fitfully blows, half conceals half discloses?
Now it catches the gleam of the morning's first beam
In full glory reflected now shines on the stream;
'Tis the Star Spangled Banner, Oh, long may it wave
O'er the land of the free and the home of the brave.

What Shall We Do With A Drunken Sailor?

Em
What shall we do with a drunken sailor?
D
What shall we do with a drunken sailor?
Em
What shall we do with a drunken sailor?
Em D   Em
Early in the morning.

Chorus:

Way, hey, and up she rises, (3 times)
Early in the morning.

Put him in the longboat till he's sober, etc.

Pull out the plug and wet him all over, etc.

Put him in the scuppers with a hose pipe on him, etc.

Heave him by the leg in a running bowline, etc.

Shave his belly with a rusty razor, etc.

Oh, thus be it ever when free men shall stand
Between their lov'd homes and the war's desolation!
Blest with vict'ry and peace,
    may the heav'n rescued land
Praise the Pow'r that hath made
    and preserved us a nation!
Then conquer we must, when our cause it is just,
And this be our motto: "In God is our trust!"
And the Star Spangled Banner in triumph shall wave
O'er the land of the free and the home of the brave.

63

Home On The Range

```
E
Oh! Give me a home where the buffalo roam,
          A
Where the deer and the antelope play;
    E    E7        A      B7
Where seldom is heard a discouraging word,
    E    B7        E
And the sky is not clouded all day.
```

Chorus:

```
E        B7        E
Home, home on the range!
    E    E7        F#      B7
Where the deer and the antelope play
    E    E7        A      Am
Where seldom is heard a discouraging word,
    E    B7        E
And the sky is not clouded all day.
```

```
E
Oh! give me the land where the bright diamond sand
Throws its light from the glittering streams,
Where glideth along the graceful white swan,
Like the maid to her heavenly dreams.
```

```
E
Oh! give me a gale of the Solomon vale
Where the lifestreams with buoyancy flow;
On the banks of the Beaver, where seldom if ever,
Any poisonous herbage doth grow.
```

```
How often at night, when the heavens were bright,
With the light of the twinkling stars,
Have I stood here amazed and asked as I gazed
If their glory exceeds that of ours.
```

The Old Gray Mare

```
                G            D  G
Oh, the old gray mare, she ain't what she used to be,
D7                         G
Ain't what she used to be, ain't what she used to be,
                    D  G
The old gray mare, she ain't what she used to be,
A7      D7  G
Many long years ago.
        C      G
Many long years ago,
A7      D7  G
Many long years ago.
                    D  G
The old gray mare, she ain't what she used to be,
A7      D7  G
Many long years ago.
```

```
The old gray mare, she kicked on the whiffletree,
Kicked on the whiffletree, kicked on the whiffletree,
The old gray mare, she kicked on the whiffletree,
Many long years ago.
Many long years ago,
Many long years ago, many long years ago,
The old gray mare, she ain't what she used to be,
Many long years ago.
```

```
I love the wild flowers in this bright land of ours,
I love the wild curlew's shrill scream;
The bluffs and white rocks and antelope flocks,
That graze on the mountain so green.
```

```
The air is so pure and the breezes so free,
The zephyrs so balmy and light,
That I would not exchange my home here to range
Forever in azures so bright.
```

64

Scarborough Fair
Derived From Child Ballad 2

Dm   Dm7   Em   Dm6
Are you going to Scarborough Fair?
Am   Dm   G   Dm
Parsley, sage, rosemary and thyme;
  Bb   Dm A7   Dm
Remember me to one that lives there,
       G   C   Dm
For once she was a true love of mine.

Tell her to make me a cambric shirt,
Parsley, sage, rosemary and thyme;
Without any seam or fine needlework,
And then she'll be a true love of mine.

Tell her to wash it in yonder dry well,
Parsley, sage, rosemary and thyme;
Where water ne'er sprung, nor drop of rain fell,
And then she'll be a true love of mine.

Tell her to dry it on yonder thorn,
Parsley, sage, rosemary and thyme;
Which never bore blossom since Adam was born,
And then she'll be a true love of mine.

Oh, will you find me an acre of land,
Parsley, sage, rosemary and thyme;
Between the sea foam and the sea sand
Or never be a true lover of mine.

Oh, will you plough it with a lamb's horn,
Parsley, sage, rosemary and thyme;
And sow it all over with one peppercorn,
Or never be a true lover of mine.

I'll Take You Home Again, Kathleen
Thomas Westendorf

        D   A7   C# D
I'll take you home again, Kathleen,
A7   A°A7   D
Across the ocean wild and wide,
       A7   C# D
To where your heart has ever been
  A   E7   D E7 A
Since first you were my bonny bride.
 A7   C# D
The roses all have left your cheek,
 A7   D
I've watched them fade away and die;
F#7 Bm   Em   F# B7
Your voice is sad when e'er you speak
E7   D E7 D E7 A
And tears be-dim your loving eyes.

Chorus:

    D   A7   C# D
Oh, I will take you back, Kathleen,
A7   A° A7   D
To where your heart will feel no pain;
           D7   G
And when the fields are fresh and green,
D°D   A7   D
I'll take you to your home again.

I know you love me, Kathleen dear,
Your heart was ever fond and true,
I always feel when you are near,
That life holds nothing, dear, but you.
The smiles that once you gave to me,
I scarcely ever see them now;
Though many times I see
A dark'ning shadow on your brow.

To that dear home beyond the sea,
My Kathleen shall again return,
And when thy old friends welcome thee,
Thy loving heart will cease to yearn.
Where laughs the little silver stream,
Beside your mother's humble cot,
And brightest rays of sunshine gleam,
There all your grief will be forgot.

The Wabash Cannonball

G
I stood on the Atlantic ocean,
          C
On the wide Pacific shore,
     D7
Heard the Queen of flowing mountains
                    G
To the South Belle by the door,
                          G
She's long, tall and handsome,
          C
She's loved by one and all.
     D7
She's a modern combination,
                    G
Called the Wabash Cannonball

Chorus:

G
Listen to the jingle,
          C
The rumble and the roar.
D7
Riding thru the woodlands,
                    G
To the hill and by the shore.
                          G
Hear the mighty rush of engines,
          C
Hear the lonesome hobo squall,
D7
Riding thru the jungles,
                    G
On the Wabash Cannonball.

Now the eastern states are dandies,
So the western people say
From New York to St. Louis
And Chicago by the way,
Thru the hills of Minnesota
Where the rippling waters fall
No chances can be taken
On the Wabash Cannonball.

Here's to Daddy Claxton,
May his name forever stand
Will he be remembered
Through parts of all our land,
When his earthly race is over
And the curtain round him falls
We'll carry him on to victory
On the Wabash Cannonball.

Nelly Bly
Stephen Foster

C   G7
Nelly Bly! Nelly Bly! Bring the broom along,
C   F
We'll sweep the kitchen clean, my dear,
G7   C
And have a little song.

Chorus:

C   F
Poke the wood, my lady love,
          G7
And make the fire burn,
C   F
And while I take the banjo down,
     G7   C
I'll sing for you and play for you
     G7   C
A dulcet melody.

C   F
Nelly Bly has a voice like a turtle dove,
I hear it in the meadow and I hear it in the grove.
Nelly Bly has a heart warm as a cup of tea,
And bigger than the sweet potatoes down in Tennessee

Nelly Bly shuts her eye when she goes to sleep.
When she wakens up again her eyeballs start to peep.
The way she walks, she lifts her foot,
     and then she bumps it down,
And when it lights, there's music there
     in that part of the town.

C   F
Heigh, Nelly! Ho, Nelly!
C   G7
Listen, love, to me,
C   F
I'll sing for you and play for you
G7   C
A dulcet melody.

Nelly Bly! Nelly Bly! Never, never sigh;
Never bring the tear drop to the corner of your eye.
For the pie is made of pumpkins
     and the mush is made of corn,
And there's corn and pumpkins plenty, love,
     a-lyin' in the barn.

66

Sweet Betsy From Pike

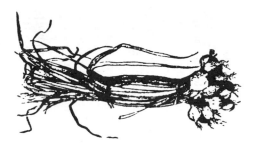

C   G7   C
Oh don't you remember sweet Betsy from Pike,
       D7   G
Who crossed the big mountains with her lover Ike,
   F   C   G7   C
With two yoke of cattle, a large yellow dog,
  Am   Dm   G7   C
A tall Shanghai rooster and a one-spotted hog.

Chorus:

         Em   G7   C
(Singin') Tooral lal looral lal looral lal la,
Em   G7   C
Tooral lal looral lal looral lal la.

One evening quite early they camped on the Platte,
'Twas near by the road on a green shady flat,
Where Betsy, sore-footed, lay down to repose,
With wonder Ike gazed on that Pike County rose.

Their wagons broke down with a terrible crash,
And out on the prairie rolled all kinds of trash;
A few little baby clothes done up with care,
'Twas rather suspicious, though all on the *square*.

The Shanghai ran off and their cattle all died,
That morning the last piece of bacon was fried;
Poor Ike was discouraged and Betsy got mad,
The dog drooped his tail and looked wondrously sad.

They stopped at Salt Lake to inquire the way,
When Brigham declared that sweet Betsy should stay;
But Betsy got frightened and ran like a deer,
While Brigham stood pawing the ground like a steer.

They soon reached the desert, where Betsy gave out,
And down in the sand she lay rolling about;
While Ike, half distracted, looked on with surprise,
Saying, "Betsy, get up, you'll get sand in your eyes."

Sweet Betsy got up in a great deal of pain,
Declared she'd go back to Pike County again;
But Ike gave a sigh, and they fondly embraced,
And they traveled along with his arm 'round her waist.

They suddenly stopped on a very high hill,
With wonder looked down upon old Placerville;
Ike sighed when he said, and he cast his eyes down,
"Sweet Betsy, my darling, we've got to Hangtown."

Long Ike and sweet Betsy attended a dance;
Ike wore a pair of his Pike County pants;
Sweet Betsy was covered with ribbons and rings;
Says Ike, "You're an angel, but where are your wings?"

A miner said, "Betsy, will you dance with me?"
"I will that, old hoss, if you don't make too free;
"But don't dance me hard, do you want to know why?
"Dog on you; I'm chock full of strong alkali!"

This Pike County couple got married of course,
But Ike became jealous, obtained a divorce;
Sweet Betsy, well satisfied, said with a great shout,
"Good-by, you big lummox, I'm glad you've backed out!"

67

Roll In My Sweet Baby's Arms

A
Ain't gonna work on the railroad,
E7
Ain't gonna work on the farm.
A
Lay 'round the shack till the mail train comes back,
      D
Then I'll roll in my sweet baby's arms.

      E7   A
Roll in my sweet baby's arms,
Roll in my sweet baby's arms,
Lay around the shack 'til the mail train comes back,
Then I'll roll in my sweet baby's arms.

Can't see what's the matter with my own true love,
She done quit writing to me;
She must think I don't love her like I used to,
Ain't that a foolish idea.

Sometimes there's a change in the ocean;
Sometimes there's a change in the sea;
Sometimes there's a change in my own true love;
But there's never no change in me.

Mama's a ginger-cake baker;
Sister can weave and can spin;
Dad's got an interest in that old cotton mill,
Just watch that old money roll in.

They tell me that your parents do not like me;
They have drove me away from your door;
If I had all my time to do over,
I would never go there any more.

Now where was you last Friday night,
While I was locked up in jail;
Walking the streets with another man,
Wouldn't even go my bail.

Old Joe Clark

E
Old Joe Clark's a fine old man,

Tell you the reason why,

He keeps good likker 'round his house,
      D   E
Good old Rock and Rye.

Chorus:

E
Fare ye well, Old Joe Clark,

Fare ye well, I say

    D   E
Fare ye well, Old Joe Clark,

I'm a-goin' away.

Old Joe Clark, the preacher's son,
Preached all over the plain,
The only text he ever knew
Was "High, low, jack and the game."

Old Joe Clark had a mule,
His name was Morgan Brown,
And every tooth in that mule's head
Was sixteen inches around.

Old Joe Clark had a yellow cat,
She would neither sing or pray,
She stuck her head in the buttermilk jar
And washed her sins away.

Old Joe Clark had a house
Fifteen stories high,
And every story in that house
Was filled with chicken pie.

I went down to old Joe's house,
He invited me to supper,
I stumped my toe on the table leg
And stuck my nose in the butter.

Now I wouldn't marry a widder,
Tell you the reason why,
She'd have so many children
They'd make those biscuits fly.

Sixteen horses in my team,
The leaders they are blind,
And every time the sun goes down
There's a pretty girl on my mind.

Eighteen miles of mountain road
And fifteen miles of sand,
If I ever travel this road again,
I'll be a married man.

Dragon Fly

In The Good Old Summertime

Ren Shields and George Evans

       G
There's a time in each year that we always hold dear,
C   G
Good old summertime.
                       D7 G
With the birds and the treeses and sweet scented breezes,
D   A7   D7
Good old summertime.
       G
When your day's work is over then you are in clover,
  C   G
And life is one beautiful rhyme,
  C   G   Edim   G
No trouble annoying, each one is enjoying
Gm6 D   A7   D7
The good old summertime.

Chorus:

       G
In the good old summertime,
G7 C   G
In the good old summertime,
              Em A7   D7
Strolling through the shady lanes with that baby mine.
       G
You hold her hand and she holds yours,
  C   G
And that's a very good sign,
           B7
That she's your tootsey-wootsey
Em A7   Am7D7G
In the good old summertime.

L'il Liza Jane

C
I've got a gal who loves me so,
F C
L'il Liza Jane,
Way down South in Baltimore,
    G7 C
L'il Liza Jane.

Chorus:

C   FC F C
Oh, E-liza, L'il Liza Jane,
      FC   G7 C
Oh, E-liza, L'il Liza Jane.

Liza Jane looks good to me,
Sweetest gal I ever see.

I fell in love when I first saw,
Now I've got me a mother-in-law.

House and lot in Baltimore,
Lots of children 'round the door.

I don't care how far I roam,
The very best place is home sweet home.

Candy Man Blues

    D
Well all you ladies gather 'round,

The good sweet candy man's in town,
              A   D
It's the candy man (candy man).

He's got a stick of candy nine-inch long,
He sells it as fast as a hog can chew corn,
It's the candy man, it's the candy man.

You all heard what Sister Jones has said,
Always takes a candy stick to bed,
It's the candy man, it's the candy man.

Don't stand close to the candy man,
He'll leave a candy stick in your hand,
It's the candy man, it's the candy man.

He sold some candy to Sister Bad,
The very next day, she took all he had,
It's the candy man, it's the candy man.

If you try his candy, good friend of mine,
You sure will want it for a long, long time,
It's the candy man, it's the candy man.

His stick candy don't melt away,
Just gets better so the ladies say,
It's the candy man, it's the candy man.

In The Evening By The Moonlight

James A. Bland

F
In the evening by the moonlight,
Bb   F
you can hear the young folks singin';
In the evening by the moonlight,
G7   C7
you can hear those banjoes ringin'.
F   F7
How the old folks would enjoy it,
    Bb   Bbm   F
they would sit all night and listen,
    Bb   F   G7   C7   F
As we sang in   the evening by the moonlight,

rah da doo day;
F
In the evening, rah da doo day;
           Bb
by the moonlight, rah da doo day,
                          F
You can hear those young folks singin', rah da doo day;

In the evening, rah da doo day,
                      by the moonlight, rah da doo day;
            G7   C7
You can hear those banjoes ringin', rah da doo day.
        F   F7
How the old folks would enjoy it,
    Bb   Bbm   F
they would sit all night and listen,
    Bb   F   G7   C7   F
As we sang in   the evening by the moonlight,
rah da doo day.

Shalom Aleichem

Hebrew

Cm G7   Cm   G7   Cm
Havenu   Shalom   Aleichem!
C7   Fm
Havenu Shalom Aleichem!
G7 Cm G7   Cm
Havenu Shalom Aleichem!
        G7
Havenu Shalom! Shalom!
                    Cm
Shalom Aleichem!

Where there's plenty of moonshine stills.

Kentucky Bootlegger

G   D   G
Come all you booze buyers, if you want to hear,
                          C   G
About the kind of booze they sell around here;
C   G
Made way back in the swamps and hills,
                        D   G
Where there's plenty of moonshine stills.

Some moonshiners make pretty good stuff.
Bootleggers use it to mix it up;
He'll make one gallon, well he'll make two,
If you don't mind boys, he'll get the best of you.

One drop will make a rabbit whip a fool dog.
And a taste will make a rabbit whip a wild hog;
It'll make a toad spit in a black snake's face,
Make a hard shell preacher fall from grace.

A lamb will lay down with a lion
After drinking that old moonshine,
So throw back your head and take a little drink,
And for a week you won't be able to think.

The moonshiners are getting mighty thick,
And the bootleggers are getting mighty slick;
If they keep on bagging, they better beware,
They'll be selling each other I do declare.

Down In The Willow Garden

E   A
Down in the willow garden
E   E   C#m
Where me and my true love did meet,
E   A
'Twas there we sat a-courting,
E B7 E
My love dropped off to sleep.
A G#m A
I had a bottle of burgundy wine
E   C#m
Which my true love did not know.
E
And there I poisoned that dear little girl
E   A   E   C#m
Down under the bank below.

I stabbed her with my dagger,
Which was a bloody knife;
I threw her in the river,
Which was a dreadful sight.
My father often told me
That money would set me free,
If I would murder that dear little girl
Whose name was Rose Connelly.

And now he sits in his cottage door,
A-wiping his weeping eye.
And now he waits for his own dear son,
Upon the scaffold high.
My race is run beneath the sun,
Cruel Hell's now waiting for me,
For I have murdered my own true love,
Whose name was Rose Connelly.

Hand Me Down My Walking Cane

G
Hand me down my walkin' cane
   D7   G
Hand me down my walkin' cane
C
Hand me down my walkin' cane,
G
I'm gonna catch the midnight train,
   D7   G
'Cause all my sins are taken away.

Oh, hand me down my bottle of corn,
I'll get drunk as sure's you're born.

Oh, I got drunk and I landed in jail,
And there wasn't no one to go my bail.

Come on, Mom, won't you go my bail,
And get me out of this Goddamn jail?

The meat is tough, and the beans are bad,
Oh, my God, I can't eat that.

If I had listened to what you said,
I'd be at home in my feather bed.

If I should die in Tennessee,
Just send my bones home C.O.D.

But if I die in New York State,
Just ship my body back by freight.

The devil chased me 'round a stump,
I thought he'd catch me at every jump.

Oh, hell is deep, and hell is wide,
Ain't got no bottom, ain't got no side.

Now some folks say, it ain't no fun,
When a song like this goes on and on.

Yes, on and on and on and on,
On and on and on and on.

71

Goodbye Old Paint

Chorus:

   A

Goodbye, old Paint, I'm a-leavin' Cheyenne,

             E7   A

Goodbye, old Paint, I'm a-leavin' Cheyenne,

Verse:

A   D   A   F#m

I'm a-leavin' Cheyenne, I'm off to Montana,

   A   E7   A

Goodbye, old Paint, I'm a-leavin' Cheyenne.

My foot in the stirrup, my pony won't stand,

And seat yourself by me so long as you stay.

Old Paint's a good pony, he paces when he can,

Goodbye, little Annie, I'm off to Cheyenne.

Oh, hitch up your horses and feed 'em some hay,

And seat yourself by me so long as you stay.

My horses ain't hungry, they'll not eat your hay,

My wagon is loaded and rolling away.

My foot in the stirrup, the reins in my hands,

Good morning, young lady, my horses won't stand.

House Of The Rising Sun

Em   B7   Em

There is a house in New Orleans,

      D   Em

They call the Rising Sun.

A   Em7   Em6

Has been the ruin of many poor girls,

Em   B7   Em

And me, oh Lord, I'm one.

My mother she's a tailor,

She sews those new blue jeans,

      Bb

My husband he's a gambling man,

Drinks down in New Orleans.

My husband he's a gambler,

He goes from town to town,

The only time he's satisfied is when

He drinks his liquor down.

Go tell my baby sister,

Never do like I have done,

Shun that house in New Orleans,

They call the Rising Sun.

One foot on the platform,

The other's on the train,

I'm going down to New Orleans,

To wear that ball and chain.

Going back to New Orleans,

My race is almost run,

I'm going to spend the rest of my life,

Beneath that Rising Sun.

I Was Born About Ten Thousand Years Ago

  F   C7

I was born about ten thousand years ago,

                              F

And there's nothing in this world that I don't know,

  Bb

I saw Peter, Paul, and Moses

               F

playing ring around the roses,

 C7   F

And I'll lick the guy who says it isn't so.

I saw Satan when he looked the garden o'er.

I saw Eve and Adam driven from the door,

When the apple they were eating

    I was 'round the corner peeking,

I can prove that I'm the guy that ate the core.

I saw Jonah when he shoved off in the whale,

And I thought he'd never live to tell the tale,

But old Jonah'd eaten garlic,

    so he gave the whale a colic

And he coughed him up and let him out of jail.

Goober Peas

```
C               F         C
Sitting by the roadside on a summer's day,
               Dm        D7 G
Chatting with my messmates, passing time away,
C             F            C
Lying in the shadow, underneath the trees,
       F    C   G7    C
Goodness how delicious, eating Goober Peas!
```

Chorus:
```
       F
Peas! Peas! Peas! Peas!
G7     C
Eating Goober Peas!
       F    C   G7    C
Goodness how delicious, eating Goober Peas!
```

When a horseman passes, the soldiers have a rule,
To cry out at their loudest, "Mister, here's your mule!"
But another pleasure enchantinger than these,
Is wearing out your grinders, eating goober peas!

Just before the battle the Gen'ral hears a row,
He says, "The Yanks are coming, I hear their rifles now."
He turns around in wonder,
    and what do you think he sees?
The Georgia Militia—eating goober peas!

I think my song has lasted almost long enough,
The subject's interesting, but rhymes are mighty rough,
I wish this war was over, when free from rags and fleas,
We'd kiss our wives and sweethearts
    and gobble goober peas!

Michael, Row The Boat Ashore

Chorus:
```
D                                 G  D
Michael, row the boat ashore, Allaluya.
             F#m     Em   A7 D
Michael, row the boat ashore, Allaluya.
```

Verses:
Michael's boat is a music boat, Allaluya, (twice

Sister help to trim the sail, Allaluya, (twice)

Jordan's River is deep and wide, Allaluya,
Meet my mother on the other side, Allaluya.

Jordan's River is chilly and cold, Allaluya,
Kills the body but not the soul, Allaluya.

Banks Of The Ohio

```
D             A7      D
I asked my love to go with me,
            A7      D
To take a walk a little way.
                     D7    G
And as we walked, and as we talked
           D  A7       D
About our golden wedding day.
```

Chorus:
Then only say that you'll be mine,
In no other arms entwine.
Down beside where the waters flow,
On the banks of the Ohio.

I asked your mother for you, dear,
And she said you were too young;
Only say that you'll be mine —
Happiness in my home you'll find.

I held a knife against her breast,
And gently in my arms she pressed,
Crying: Willie, oh Willie, don't murder me,
For I'm unprepared for eternity.

I took her by her lily white hand,
Led her down where the waters stand.
I picked her up and I pitched her in,
Watched her as she floated down.

I started back home twixt twelve and one,
Crying, My God, what have I done?
I've murdered the only woman I love,
Because she would not be my bride.

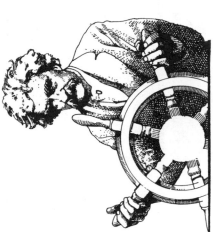

Grandfather's Clock

Henry Clay Work

```
  G          D7      G        C
My grandfather's clock was too large for the shelf,
  G        D7     G        C
So it stood ninety years on the floor;
        D7    G        C
It was taller by half than the old man himself,
   G        D7       G
Though it weighed not a pennyweight more.
   G              D7         G
It was bought on the morn of the day that he was born,
              A7            D7
And was always his treasure and pride;
   G       D7    G       C
But it stopped short never to go again
     G   D7   G
When the old man died.
```

Chorus:

```
      G
Ninety years without slumbering,

      D7               G
Tick tock, tick tock,

His life seconds numbering,

      D7   G           C
Tick tock, tick tock,

   D7  G       C
It stopped short never to go again
     G   D7   G
When the old man died.
```

In watching its pendulum swing to and fro,
Many hours had he spent while a boy;
And in childhood and manhood the clock seemed to know,
And to share both his grief and his joy.
For it struck twenty-four when he entered at the door,
With a blooming and beautiful bride, etc.

My grandfather said that of those he could hire,
Not a servant so faithful he found;
For it wasted no time, and had but one desire,
At the close of each-week to be wound.
And it kept in its place, not a frown upon its face,
And its hands never hung by its side, etc.

It rang an alarm in the dead of the night,
An alarm that for years had been dumb;
And we knew that his spirit was pluming its flight,
That his hour of departure had come.
Still the clock kept the time, with a soft and muffled chime,
As we silently stood by his side, etc.

Ida Red

```
  G
Ida Red, Ida Green,
            D7  G
Purtiest gal I ever seen.
```

Ida Red lives in town,
Weighs three hundred and forty pounds.

```
  G
Ida Red, Ida Red,
                D7
I'm just crazy 'bout Ida Red.
```

Ida Red, Ida Blue,
Ida bit a hoecake half in two.

Ida Red, Ida Red,
Everybody's crazy 'bout Ida Red.

If I'd a-listened to what Ida said,
I'd a-been sleeping in Ida's bed.

The Streets Of Laredo

    D   A7   D   A7
As I walked out in the streets of Laredo,
  D   A7   D   A7
As I walked out in Laredo one day,
  D   A7   D   A7
I spied a poor cowboy wrapped up in white linen,
  D   G   A7   D
All wrapped in white linen and cold as the clay.

"I see by your outfit that you are a cowboy,"
These words he did say as I proudly stepped by,
"Come sit down beside me and hear my sad story,
Got shot in the breast and I know I must die.

"'Twas once in the saddle I used to go dashing,
'Twas once in the saddle I used to go gay;
'Twas first to drinkin', and then to card-playing,
Got shot in the breast and I'm dying today.

"Let six jolly cowboys come carry my coffin,
Let six pretty gals come carry my pall;
Throw bunches of roses all over my coffin,
Throw roses to deaden the clods as they fall.

"Oh, beat the drum slowly, and play the fife lowly,
And play the dead march as you carry me along,
Take me to the green valley and lay the earth o'er me,
For I'm a poor cowboy and I know I've done wrong."

Oh we beat the drum slowly and we played the fife lowly,
And bitterly wept as we carried him along,
For we all loved our comrade,
  so brave, young and handsome,
We all loved our comrade although he done wrong.

Old Dan Tucker
Dan Emmett

           G
Now old Dan Tucker's a fine old man,
           D7
Washed his face in a fryin' pan,
  G
Combed his head with a wagon wheel,
                  D7
And died with a toothache in his heel.

Chorus:

 G   C
Get out the way, old Dan Tucker,
D7   G
You're too late to get your supper.
            C
Get out the way old Dan Tucker,
D7   G
You're too late to get your supper.

Now old Dan Tucker is come to town,
Riding a billy goat—leading a hound,
Hound dog bark and the billy goat jump,
Landed Dan Tucker on top of the stump.

Now old Dan Tucker he got drunk,
Fell in the fire and kicked up a chunk,
Red hot coal got in his shoe,
And oh my lawd how the ashes flew.

Now old Dan Tucker is come to town,
Swinging the ladies round and round,
First to the right and then to the left,
Then to the girl that he loves best.

In The Pines

     Em   Am Em
True love, true love, don't lie to me,
        B7   Em
Tell me where did you sleep last night?

              Am   Em
In the pines, in the pines,
Where the sun never shines,
B7   Em
I shivered the whole night through.

                                                                                                    ?
True love, true love, where did you go?
I went where the cold wind blows,
In the pines, in the pines,
Where the sun never shines,
And I shivered the whole night through.

My husband was a railroad man,
Killed a mile and a half from town,
His head was found
In a driver's wheel,
And his body has never been found.

True love, true love, don't lie to me,
Tell me, where'd you sleep last night?
In the pines, in the pines,
Where the sun never shines,
And I shivered the whole night through.

Git Along, Little Dogies

F   G   C
As I was a-walking one morning for pleasure,
F   G   C
I spied a cowpuncher a-riding along;
      Dm7   Em   Am
His hat was throwed back and his spurs were a-jinglin',
C   F   G7   C
As he approached me singin' this song:

Chorus:

   Gm7   C   F
Whoopee ti yi yo, git along, little dogies,
C   Am   Dm7   G
It's your misfortune and none of my own;
C   Em   Am
Whoopee ti yi yo, git along, little dogies,
C   F   Em   C
For you know Wyoming will be your new home.

Early in the springtime we'll round up the dogies,
Slap on their brands and bob off their tails;
Round up our horses, load up the chuck wagon,
Then throw those dogies upon the trail.

It's whooping and yelling and driving the dogies,
Oh, how I wish you would go on,
It's whooping and punching and go on, little dogies,
For you know Wyoming will be your new home.

Some of the boys goes up the trail for pleasure,
But that's where they git it most awfully wrong;
For you haven't any idea the trouble they give us,
When we go driving them dogies along.

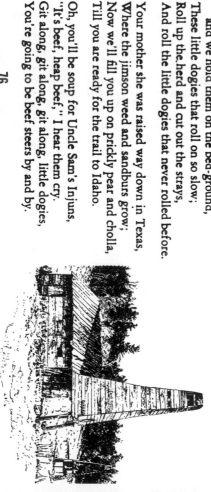

My Home's Across The Smokey Mountains

     D
My home's across the Smokey Mountains,
A7   D
My home's across the Smokey Mountains,
     A7   D
My home's across the Smokey Mountains,
     A7   D
And I'll never get to see you any more, more, more,
     A7   D
I'll never get to see you any more.

Goodbye honey, sugar darlin', (3 times)
And I'll never get to see you any more, more, more,
I'll never get to see you any more.

Rock my baby, feed her candy, (3 times)
And I'll never get to see you any more, more, more,
I'll never get to see you any more.

When the night comes on
    and we hold them on the bed-ground,
These little dogies that roll on so slow;
Roll up the herd and cut out the strays,
And roll the little dogies that never rolled before.

Your mother she was raised way down in Texas,
Where the jimson weed and sandburs grow;
Now we'll fill you up on prickly pear and cholla,
Till you are ready for the trail to Idaho.

Oh, you'll be soup for Uncle Sam's Injuns,
"It's beef, heap beef," I hear them cry.
Git along, git along, git along, little dogies,
You're going to be beef steers by and by.

I Ride An Old Paint

G
I ride an old paint and I lead an old Dan,
   D7   G
I'm goin' to Montana to throw the Hoolian,
   D7   G
They feed 'em in the coulees, they water in the draw,
   D7   G
Their tails are all matted, their backs are all raw.

Chorus:

   D7
Ride around little doggies,
   G
Ride around them slow,
   D7
For the fiery and snuffy
   G
Are raring to go.

Old Bill Jones had a daughter and a son,
Son went to college and the daughter went wrong,
His wife got killed in a pool-room fight,
Still he keeps singing from morning till night.

When I die take my saddle from the wall,
Put it on to my pony, lead him out of his stall,
Tie my bones to his back, turn our faces to the west,
And we'll ride the prairie that we love the best.

Muskrat

G
Muskrat, oh, muskrat,

What makes you smell so bad?

I've been in the bottom all my life
        C   G
Till I'm mortified in my head, head, head,
        C   G
Till I'm mortified in my head.

Rattlesnake, oh, rattlesnake,
What makes your teeth so white?
I've been in the bottom all my life
And I ain't done nothin' but bite, bite, etc.

Groundhog, oh, groundhog,
What makes your back so brown?
It's a wonder I don't smotherfy,
Livin' down in the ground, ground, etc.

Rooster, oh, rooster,
What makes your claws so hard?
Been scratchin' this gravel all my days,
It's a wonder I ain't tired, etc.

Jaybird, oh, jaybird,
What makes you fly so high?
Been robbin' your cornpatch all my life,
It's a wonder I don't die, die, etc.

Yankee Doodle

G   D7
Yankee Doodle went to town,
    G   D7
A-riding on a pony;
G   C
Stuck a feather in his hat
       D7   G
And called it macaroni.

Chorus:

C
Yankee Doodle keep it up,
G
Yankee Doodle dandy,
C
Mind the music and the step
      G   D7   G
And with the girls be handy.

Father and I went down to camp
Along with Captain Gooding;
And there we saw the men and boys,
As thick as hasty pudding.

There was Captain Washington
Upon a slapping stallion,
A-giving orders to his men,
I guess there was a million.

And there we saw a thousand men,
As rich as 'Squire David;
And what they wasted every day,
I wish it could be sa-ved.

John Henry

E
When John Henry was a little baby,
B7
Sitting on his papa's knee,
A7
Well he picked up a hammer and little piece of steel,
E   B7   E
Said "Hammer's gonna be the death of me, Lord, Lord;
E   A7
"Hammer's gonna be the death of me."

The captain said to John Henry,
"I'm gonna bring that steam drill around,
"I'm gonna bring that steam drill out on the job,
"I'm gonna whup that steel on down."
(Lord, Lord!)

John Henry told his captain,
"Lord a man ain't nothing but a man,
But before I'd let your steam drill beat me down,
I'd die with a hammer in my hand!"
(Lord, Lord)

John Henry said to his shaker,
"Shaker why don't you sing?
Because I'm swinging thirty pounds
from my hips on down;
Just listen to that cold steel ring."
(Lord, Lord)

Now the captain said to John Henry,
"I believe that mountain's caving in."
John Henry said right back to the captain,
"Ain't nothing but my hammer sucking wind."
(Lord, Lord)

Now the man that invented the steam drill,
He thought he was mighty fine;
But John Henry drove fifteen feet,
The steam drill only made nine.
(Lord, Lord)

John Henry hammered in the mountains,
His hammer was striking fire,
But he worked so hard, it broke his poor heart
And he laid down his hammer and he died.
(Lord, Lord)

Now John Henry had a little woman,
Her name was Polly Anne,
John Henry took sick and had to go to bed,
Polly Anne drove steel like a man.
(Lord, Lord)

John Henry had a little baby,
You could hold him in the palm of your hand;
And the last words I heard that poor boy say,
"My daddy was a steel driving man."
(Lord, Lord)

So every Monday morning
When the blue birds begin to sing,
You can hear John Henry a mile or more;
You can hear John Henry's hammer ring.
(Lord, Lord)

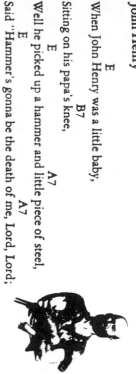

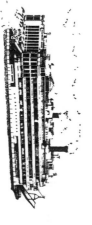

78

Shenandoah

D   G   D
Oh, Shenandoah, I long to see you,
G   A7   D
Away, you rolling river.
G   F#m   Bm
Oh, Shenandoah, I long to see you,
D
Away, I'm bound away,' cross
G   D
The wide Missouri.

O, Shenandoah, I love your daughter,
Away, etc.
O, Shenandoah, I love your daughter,
Away, we're bound, etc.

O, Shenandoah, I long to see you,
O, Shenandoah, I'll not deceive you,

O, seven years, I've been a rover,
For seven years I've been a rover,

Wandering

D   G7
I've been a wandering early and late,

New York City to the Golden Gate,
```
            A7
```
And it looks like
```
    G7        Bb      D
```
I'm never gonna cease my wandering.

Been working in the army, working on a farm,
All I got to show for it's just this muscle in my arm,
And it looks like
I'm never gonna cease my wandering.

There's snakes on the mountain, there's eels in the sea,
Red-headed woman made a fool out of me,
And it looks like
I'm never gonna cease my wandering.

My daddy is an engineer, my brother drives a hack,
Sister takes in washing and the baby balls the jack,
And it looks like
I'm never gonna cease my wandering.

They may sing of their roses which by other names,
Would smell just as sweetly, they say,
But I know that my Rose would never consent
To have that sweet name taken away.
Her glances are shy when e'er I pass by
The bower where my true love grows.
And my one wish has been that some day I may win
The heart of my wild Irish rose.

My Wild Irish Rose
Chauncey Olcott

```
       C        C5#     F      C
```
If you listen, I'll sing you a sweet little song
```
                    D        G7
```
Of a flower that's now drooped and dead,
```
     C      C5#    F     C
```
Yet dearer to me, yes than all of its mates,
```
    C      Fm       C
```
Tho' each holds aloft its proud head.
```
  G7                      C
```
'Twas given to me by a girl that I know;
```
         Am        D7        G7
```
Since we've met, faith, I've known no repose,
```
   C      C5#       F
```
She is dearer by far than the world's brightest star,
```
   C        F      C
```
And I call her my wild Irish rose.

Chorus:

```
  C    Fm    C     F       C
```
My wild Irish rose, the sweetest flow'r that grows,
```
    G7      C    C#dim G7          C
```
You may search ev'rywhere, but none can compare
```
   Am    D  D7  G7
```
with my wild Irish rose.
```
   C    Fm   C     F       C
```
My wild Irish rose, the dearest flow'r that grows,
```
C#dim  G7     C   C#dim G7        C
```
And some day for my sake, she may let me take
```
  F     C  D7  G7  C
```
the bloom from my wild Irish rose.

A Bicycle Built For Two (Daisy Bell)

Harry Dacre

```
F                              C7          Gm7   C7  F
There is a flower within my heart, Daisy, Daisy!
                                   C7
Planted one day by a glancing dart,
F       C  C7  F
Planted by Daisy Bell!
Dm             A7         Dm
Whether she loves me or loves me not,
Gm              Bb 7   A7
Sometimes it's hard to    tell;
Dm      A7    Dm        G7            C
Yet I am longing to share the lot of beautiful Daisy Bell!
```

Chorus:

```
F                           Bb                      F
Daisy, Daisy, give me your answer, do!
C7      F    Gm7      G7              C7
I'm half crazy, all for the love of you!
D Gm       C     C7  F
It won't be a stylish marriage,
C F     Bb         F
I can't afford a carriage
C7 F    C7    F   C
But you'll look sweet on the seat
       F   Gm7 C7 F
Of a bicycle built for two
```

```
We will go "tandem" as man and wife, Daisy, Daisy!
"Peddling" away down the road of life,
I and my Daisy Bell!
When the road's dark we can both despise
P'licemen and "lamps" as well;
There are "bright lights" in the dazzling eyes
   of beautiful Daisy Bell!
```

```
I will stand by you in "wheel" or woe, Daisy, Daisy!
You'll be the bell(e) which I'll ring, you know!
Sweet little Daisy Bell!
You'll take the "lead" in each "trip" we take,
Then, if I don't do well,
I will permit you to use the brake, my beautiful Daisy Bell!
```

Who's Gonna Shoe Your Pretty Little Foot?

```
C
Who's gonna shoe your pretty little foot?
F                     C
Who's gonna glove your hand?
F                          C
Who's gonna kiss your red ruby lips?
     G7      C
Who's gonna be your man?
```

```
F
Papa will shoe my pretty little foot,
Mama will glove my hand,
Sister's gonna kiss my red ruby lips,
I don't need no man.
```

```
I don't need no man, poor boy,
I don't need no man.
Sister's gonna kiss my red ruby lips
I don't need no man.
```

```
Longest train I ever did see,
Was sixteen coaches long.
The only girl I ever did love,
Was on that train and gone.
```

80

Old Folks At Home
Stephen Foster

C   F
Way down upon the Swanee River,
C G7
Far, far away,
C   F
There's where my heart is turning ever,
C G7 C
There's where the old folks stay.
C   F
All up and down the whole creation,
C G7
Sadly I roam,
C   F
Still longing for the old plantation,
C G7 C
And for the old folks at home.

Chorus:

G7 C
All the world is sad and dreary
F G7
Everywhere I roam;
C   F
Oh, brothers, how my heart grows weary,
C G7 C
Far from the old folks at home.

All roun' the little farm I wandered,
When I was young;
Then many happy days I squandered,
Many the songs I sung.
When I was playing with my brother,
Happy was I;
Oh! take me to my kind old mother,
There let me live and die.

I'm Going Down This Road Feeling Bad

   E   E7
I'm going down this road feeling bad,
   A   E
I'm going down this road feeling bad,
   A   E
I'm going down this road feeling bad, Lord Lord,
     B7   E
And I ain't gonna be treated this a-way.

I'm down in that jail on my knees, (twice)
I'm down in that jail on my knees, Lord, Lord,
I ain't gonna be treated this-a-way.

They fed me on cornbread and beans, etc.
Takes a ten dollar shoe to fit my feet, etc.
'Cause your two dollar shoes hurt my feet, etc.
I'm going where the weather suits my clothes, etc.
That's why I'm going down this road feeling bad, etc.

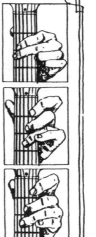

One little hut among the bushes,
One that I love,
Still sadly to my mem'ry rushes,
No matter where I rove.
When will I see the bees a-humming
All roun' the comb?
When will I hear the banjo strumming,
Down in my good old home?

This Old Man

C
This old man, he played one,
F   G
He played knick-knack on my thumb,
     C
With a knick-knack, paddy wack,

Give the dog a bone,
G7   C
This old man came rolling home.

This old man, he played two,
He played knick-knack on my shoe, etc.

This old man, he played three,
He played knick-knack on my knee, etc.

This old man, he played four,
He played knick-knack on my door, etc.

This old man, he played five,
He played knick-knack on my hive, etc.

This old man, he played six,
He played knick-knack on my sticks, etc.

This old man, he played seven,
He played knick-knack up in heaven, etc.

This old man, he played eight,
He played knick-knack on my gate, etc.

This old man, he played nine,
He played knick-knack on my vine, etc.

This old man, he played ten,
He played knick-knack all over again, etc.

Take A Whiff On Me

Chorus:

      G
Take a whiff, take a whiff, take a whiff on me,
C
Ev'rybody take a whiff on me,
D7   G
Hey, hey, baby take a whiff on me.

Take a whiff, take a whiff, take a whiff on me,
C
Ev'rybody take a whiff on me,
D7   G
Hey, hey, baby take a whiff on me.

Verses:

G
I got a woman six feet tall,
C
Sleepin' in the kitchen with her feet in the hall,
D7   G
Hey, hey, baby take a whiff on me.

Two old maids a-fishin' in the creek,
They ain't caught a man since a-way last week,
Hey, hey, baby take a whiff on me.

Want to get a woman let me tell you a word,
Grease your hair down as slick as lard,
Hey, hey, baby take a whiff on me.

I'm a-walkin' down the road with my hat in my hand,
Lookin' for a woman who needs a worried man,
Hey, hey, baby take a whiff on me.

Horse Fly

Take This Hammer

      C   G7
Take this hammer, carry it to the captain
                        C
Take this hammer, carry it to the captain,
                           F
Take this hammer, carry it to the captain
      C   G7   C
Tell him I'm a-gone, tell him I'm gone.

If he asks you, was I running (3 times)
Tell him I was flying.

If he asks you, was I laughing (3 times)
Tell him I was crying.

I don't want no cornbread and 'lasses (3 times)
It hurts my pride.

Walkin' down the road, the road is mighty muddy,
Slippin' and slidin' and I can't stand steady,
Hey, hey, baby take a whiff on me.

I know my woman ain't a-treatin' me right,
She don't get home till the day gets light
Hey, hey, baby take a whiff on me.

Meet a lot of women out a-ramblin' around,
But the Boston women are the best that I found,
Hey, hey, baby take a whiff on me.

Sing your song all night long,
Sing to my woman from midnight on,
Hey, hey, baby take a whiff on me. 82

SONGS from around the WORLD

Ah! Si Mon Moine Voulait Danser
Quebec

G   D7   G
Ah! Si mon moine voulait danser!
     D7   G
Ah! Si mon moine voulait danser!
      D7   G
Un capuchon je lui donnerais!
      D7   G
Un capuchon je lui donnerais!

Chorus:

Danse, mon moin', danse!

Tu n'entends pas la danse!
         D7   G
Tu n'entends pas mon moulin, lon la!
         D7   G
Tu n'entends pas mon moulin marcher!

Ah! Si mon moine voulais danser! (twice)
Un ceinturon je lui donnerais! (twice)

Ah! Si mon moine voulait danser! (twice)
Un chapelet je lui donnerais! (twice)

S'il n'avait fait voue de pauverte! (twice)
Bien d'autres chos' je lui donnerais! (twice)

Cielito Lindo
Mexico

A   E7   A
De la Sierra Morena,
  E7   A   E7
Cielito Lindo vienen bajando.

                A
Un par de ojitos negros,

Cielito Lindo, los contrabando.

Chorus:

         D   Bm
Ay, ay, ay, ay
  E7   A
Canta y no llores,
                Bm
Porque cantando se a legran,
  E7   A
Cielito Lindo los corazones.

Una flecha en el aire,
Cielito Lindo, lanzó Cupido
Y como fué jugando,
Cielito Lindo, yo fuí el herido.

Du, Du Liegst Mir Im Herzen
Germany

C   G7
Du, du liegst mir im Herzen,
            C
Du, du liegst mir im Sinn;
               G7
Du, du machst mir viel Schmerzen,
                  C
Weisst nicht wie gut ich dir bin;
F   C   G7 C
Ja, Ja, ja,   ja
G7   C
Weisst nicht wie gut ich dir bin.

So, so wie ich dich liebe,
So, so liebe auch mich!
Die, die zärtlichsten Triebe
Fühl ich allein nur für dich.
Ja, ja, ja, ja,
Fühl ich allein, etc.

Doch, doch darf ich dir trauen,
Dir, dir mit leichtem Sinn?
Du, du darfst auf mich bauen,
Weisst ja, wie gut ich dir bin!....

Und, und wenn in der Ferne,
Dir, dir mein Bild erscheint,
Dann, dann wünscht ich so gerne,
Dass uns die Liebe vereint!....

83

Frère Jacques
(Brother John)
French

```
F   C7 F      C7 F
Frère Jacques,  frère Jacques
   C7  F     C7  F
Dormez-vous, dormez-vous,
      C7    F     C7   F
Sonnez les matines, sonnez les matines,
    C7  F    C7  F
Din, din, don, din, din, don.
```

Singable Translation:

Are you sleeping, are you sleeping,
Brother John, Brother John?
Morning bells are ringing, morning bells are ringing,
Ding ding dong, ding ding dong.

Sur Le Pont D'Avignon
(On The Bridge At Avignon)
France

Refrain:

```
G          D7
Sur le pont d'Avignon,
G             D7
L'on y danse, l'on y danse,
G          D7
Sur le pont d'Avignon,
G         D7  G
L'on y danse tout en rond!

G                     D7   G
Les beaux messieurs font comm' çi,
         D7     G
Et puis encor' comm' ça.
```

Les belles dam's font comm' çi,
Et puis encor' comm' ça.

Les militair's font comm' çi,
Et puis encor' comm' ça.

Singable Translation:

On the bridge at Avignon,
See them dancing, see them dancing,
On the bridge at Avignon,
See them dancing round and round!

Gentlemen bow this way,
Then again bow that way.

Ladies all bow this way,
Then again bow that way.

Soldiers, they bow this way,
Then again bow that way.

Shalom Chaverim
Hebrew

```
Dm
Shalom chaverim, shalom chaverim,
Shalom, shalom,
L'hit ra-ot, l'hit ra-ot,
Shalom, shalom.
```

Singable Translation:

Glad tidings we bring of peace on earth,
Good will towards men,
Of peace on earth, of peace on earth,
Good will towards men.

Hava Nagila
Israel

```
E                          Am     E
Hava nagila, hava nagila, hava nagila V' nism'cha.
                           Am     E
Hava nagila, hava nagila, hava nagila V' nism'cha.
Dm
Hava n' ran'na, hava n' ran'na,
E
hava n' ran' na, v' nism'cha.
Dm
Hava n' ran' na, hava n' ran'na,
E
hava n' ran'na, v' nism'cha.
Am                                                Dm
Uru, uru achim, uru a chim b'lev sameach, uru a chim
E              E7    Am
b'lev sameach,
Uru a chim uru a chim b'lev sameach.
```

O Canada!

Words: Adolphe Routhier, Music: Calixa Lavilee
English Text: Stanley Weir

Quebec

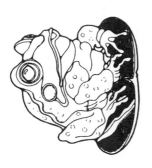

```
D A7  Bm  A7 D       A7
O Canada! Terre de nos aieux,
D   E7    A    Bm  A       E7   A
Ton front est ceint de fleurons glorieux!
     A7                        D
Car ton bras sait porter l'épée,
  G       E7 A
Il  sait  porter  la  croix!
       A7            D   E ♭ dim
Ton histoire est une épopée.
   A    E7     A
Des plus brillants exploits.
D   A7   Bm  Em        A
Et  ta  valeur, de  foi  trempee,
D Daug G       Bm Em F
Protégera  nos  foyers  et  nos  droits,
D Daug G       D A7 D
Protégera nos foyers et nos droits.
```

Sous l'oeil de Dieu, près du fleuve géant,
Le Canadien grandit en espérant,
Il est né d'une race fière,
Béni fut son berceau.
Le ciel a marque sa carrière,
Dans ce monde nouveau.
Toujours guidé pras sa lumiére,
Il garders l'honneur de son drapeau. (twice)

De son patron, précurseur du vrai Dieu,
Il porte au front l'auréole de feu.
Ennemi de la tyrannie,
Mais plein de loyauté,
Il veut garder dans l'harmonie
Sa fière liberté;
Et par l'effort de son génie,
Sur notre sol asseoir la verité. (twice)

Amour sacré du trône de l'autel,
Remplis nos coeurs de ton souffle immortel!
Parmi les races étrangères,
Notre guide est la loi:
Sachons être un peiple de freres
Sous le joug de la foi.
Et répétons, comme nos pères,
Le cri vainqueur "Pour le Christ et le Roi! (twice)

Singable Translation:

O Canada! Our home and native land,
True patriot love in all thy sons command.
With glowing hearts we see thee rise,
The true North strong and free;
And stand on guard, O Canada,
We stand on guard for thee.
O Canada! glorious and free!
O Canada! We stand on guard for thee!

O Canada! Where pines and maples grow,
Great prairies spread and lordly rivers flow.
How dear to us thy vast domain,
From East to Western sea,
Thou land of hope for all who toil,
Thou true North, strong and free!

O Canada! Beneath thy shining skies
May stalwart sons and gentle maidens rise;
To keep thee steadfast through the years
From East to Western sea,
Our Fatherland, our Motherland!
Our true North strong and free!

Ruler Supreme, Who hearest humble pray'r,
Hold our dominions all Thy loving care.
Help us to find, O God, in Thee,
A lasting, rich reward,
As waiting for the better day
We ever stand on guard.

Ragupati Ragava Rajah Ram

India; Hindu hymn

Refrain:

E
Ragupati ragava rajah Ram

E
Puhtita bhavana si ta ram.

Verses:

Em
Si ta ram je si ta ram,

Puhtita bhavana si ta ram.

Ishere Allah tere nam

Tubko sunmutti de bhagawan.

Literal Translation:

Oh God! Please give good counsel
To us who may call you Ishere
And to us who may call you Allah
And lead us properly.

South Australia

     C   F C
In South Australia, I was born,

F C F C
Heave away, haul away,

         G   Am
In South Australia, 'round Cape Horn,

C   G7 C
We're bound for South Australia.

Chorus:

             F C
Haul away your rolling king,

F   F   C
Heave away, haul away,

               Am
Haul away, oh hear me sing,

C   G7 C
We're bound for South Australia.

As I walked out one morning fair, etc.
'Twas there I met Miss Nancy Blair, etc.

I shook her up, I shook her down
I shook her round and round the town.

There ain't but one thing grieves my mind,
To leave Miss Nancy Blair behind.

And as we wallop around Cape Horn,
You'll wish to God you'd never been born.

Santa Lucia

Italy

C   G7   C
Now 'neath the silver moon ocean, is glowing,

C   G7   C
O'er the calm billows, soft winds are blowing.

C   G7   C
Here balmy breezes blow, pure joys invite us,

             G7   C
And as we gently row, all things delight us.

Chorus:

          F   C
Hark, how the sailor's cry joyously echoes night:

       G7   C
Santa Lucia, Santa Lucia!

        F   C
Home of fair poesy, realm of pure harmony,

   G7   C
Santa Lucia, Santa Lucia!

When o'er the waters light winds are playing,
Thy spell can soothe us, all care allaying.
To thee sweet Napoli, what charms are given,
Where smiles creation, toil blest by heaven.

Hava Na Shira

Hebrew

      A   E A D   A   E7
I. Hava na Shira Shire Hallelujah.

      A   E A D   A   E7 A
II. Hava na Shira Shire Hallelujah.

       A   E A D   A   E7 A
III. Hava na Shira Shire Hallelujah.

Suliram
Indonesia

```
      C        G7
Suliram, suliram, ram, ram,
  C    F    C    F    C    G7   C
Suliram yang manis Aduhai indung suher rang
         G7                 C
Bidjalka sana di pandang manis
     Am G C   G7
La suliram, suliram, ram, ram,
  C    F    C    F    C    G7   C
Suliram yang manis Aduhai indung suher rang
         G7                 C
Bidjalka sana di pandang manis.

            C    G    C
Tingi la tingi, si mata hari.
Am G C            F         C
Suliram. Anakla koorbau mati toor-tam-bat.
Am G C   F    C G7   C
Suliram. Sudala lama saiya menchari.
         G7             C
Baruse klarung saiya mendabat.
     Am G C
La suliram, etc.
```

Tumbalalaika
Yiddish

```
Am                       E7
Shtayt a bocher un er tracht
                              Am
Tracht un tracht die gantze nacht.

Vemen tzu nemen un nit farshemen,
Dm      E7       Am
Vemen tzu nemen un nit farshemen.
```

Chorus:

```
Am                              E7
Tumbala, tumbala, tumbala-lai-ka.
                                Am
Tumbala tumbala, tumbala-lai-ka
                   Dm      Am
Tumbala lai-ka, shpiel balalaika,
   Dm       E7              Am
Tumbala-lai-ka, fraylach zol zain.

Maydl, maydl, 'chvel bai dir fregn,
Vos ken vaksn, vaksn on regn,
Vos ken brenen un nit oifhern,
Vos ken benken, vaynen on trern.

Narishe bocher, vos darfst du fregn,
A shtayn ken vaksn, vaksn on regn,
A liebe ken brenen un nit oifhern,
A hartz ken benken, vaynen on trern.
```

Zum Gali Gali
Israel

```
Em
Zum gali gali gali, zum gali gali, zum gali gali
Hechalutz le'man avodah
Zum gali gali, Zum gali gali gali, zum gali gali gali
Avodah le man hecahlutz.
Zum gali gali, zum gali gali.
```

Literal Translation:

A youth worries all night long about whether he can overcome his shyness enough to find himself a girl.

(The youth speaks:) "Maiden, I would ask you: What can grow without rain; what can burn without burning itself out; and what can cry without tears?"

(The maiden replies:) "Foolish boy, how can you be so stupid? A stone (implying nothing) can grow without rain; love can burn without burning itself out; and a heart can cry without tears."

87

SONGS of the CHURCH

Amazing Grace

G   Bm   C   G
Amazing grace, how sweet the sound,
          A7 D
That saved a wretch like me.
    G   C   G
I once was lost, but now am found
   Em   G   D7 G
Was blind, but now I see,

'Twas grace that taught my heart to fear,
And grace my fears relieved;
How precious did that grace appear
The hour I first believed.

Thro' many dangers, toils and snares,
I have already come;
'Tis grace hath bro't me safe thus far,
And grace will lead me home.

How sweet the name of Jesus sounds
In a believer's ear.
It soothes his sorrows, heals his wounds,
And drives away his fear.

Must Jesus bear the cross alone
And all the world go free?
No, there's a cross for ev'ry one
And there's a cross for me.

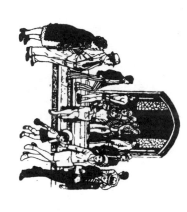

Beulah Land
Edgar Page and John R. Sweeney

  E
I've reached the land of corn and wine,
    B7   E
And all its riches freely mine;
           B7 C#m
Here shines undimmed one blissful day,
  A6   B7   E
For all my night has passed away.

Chorus:

  B   E
Oh, Beulah Land, sweet Beulah Land,
E7 A   B7   E
As on thy highest mount I stand,
  A6   C# F#m
I look away across the sea,
B7   E
Where mansions are prepared for me,
E7 A   A7 E
And view the shining glory shore,
  A6   B7   E
My heav'n, my home forevermore.

The Saviour comes and walks with me,
And sweet communion here have we;
He gently leads me with His hand,
For this is heaven's borderland.

A sweet perfume upon the breeze
Is borne from ever vernal trees,
And flow'rs that never fading grow
Where streams of life forever flow.

Went back home, Lord, my home was lonesome
Since my mother she was gone:
All my brothers, sisters crying,
What a home so sad and lone.

Bringing In The Sheaves

Knowles Shaw and George A. Minor

Sowing in the morning, sowing seeds of kindness,
Sowing in the noontide and dewy eves;
Waiting for the harvest, and the time of reaping,
We shall come, rejoicing, bringing in the sheaves.

Chorus:
Bringing in the sheaves, bringing in the sheaves,
We shall come, rejoicing, bringing in the sheaves;
Bringing in the sheaves, bringing in the sheaves,
We shall come, rejoicing, bringing in the sheaves.

Sowing in the sunshine, sowing in the shadows,
Fearing neither clouds nor winter's chilling breeze;
By and by the harvest, and the labor ended,
We shall come, rejoicing, bringing in the sheaves.

Going forth with weeping, sowing for the Master,
Tho' the loss sustained our spirit often grieves;
When our weeping's over, He will bid us welcome,
We shall come, rejoicing, bringing in the sheaves.

Can The Circle Be Unbroken?

E
I was standing by the window
      A   E
On one cold and cloudy day;

And I saw the hearse come rolling
      B7
For to carry my mother away.

Chorus:
E
O, can the circle be unbroken?
    A   E
Bye and bye, Lord, bye and bye.

There's a better home a-waiting
    B7   E
In the sky, Lord, in the sky.

Lord, I told the undertaker,
"Undertaker, please drive slow;
For this body you are hauling,
Lord, I hate to see her go."

I followed close behind her,
Tried to hold up and be brave;
But I could not hide my sorrow
When they laid her in the grave.

Get On Board, Little Children

Chorus:

G   C
Get on board, little children,
      G
Get on board, little children,
      C
Get on board, little children,
   G   D7   G
There's room for many a more.

Verses:

   G
The gospel train's a-comin',
      D7
I hear it just at hand,
G   C
I hear the car wheels rumblin'
  G   D7   G
And rollin' through the land.

I hear that train a-comin',
She's comin' 'round the curve,
She's loosened all her steam and brakes
And straining every nerve.

The fare is cheap and all can go,
The rich and poor are there,
No second class aboard this train,
No difference in the fare.

Give Me That Old Time Religion

G
Give me that old time religion,
D7
Give me that old time religion,
G   C
Give me that old time religion,
G   D7 G
It's good enough for me.

It was good for my father, etc.

It was good for my mother, etc.

It was good for the Hebrew children....

It was good for Paul and Silas, etc.

Jacob's Ladder

D
We are climbing Jacob's ladder,
A7   D
We are climbing Jacob's ladder,
G   D
We are climbing Jacob's ladder,
A7   D
Soldiers of the Cross.

D
We are climbing Jacob's ladder,
A7   D
We are climbing Jacob's ladder,
Soldiers of the Cross.

Every rung goes higher, higher, (3 times)
Soldiers of the Cross.

Sinner, do you love your Jesus?, etc.

If you love Him, why not serve Him?, etc.

Do you think I'd make a soldier?, etc.

We are climbing higher and higher, etc.

I Am A Pilgrim

D7   G
I am a pilgrim, and a stranger,
C   G
Traveling through this wearisome land;
D7 G   G7   C
I got a home in that yonder city, oh Lord,
G   D7   G
And it's not made, not made by hand.

I got a mother, a sister, and a brother,
Who have gone to that sweet land.
I'm determined to go and see them, good Lord,
All over on that distant shore.

As I go down to that river of Jordan,
Just to bathe my weary soul,
If I could touch but the hem of His garment, good Lord,
Well, I believe it would make me whole.

He's Got The Whole World In His Hands

F   B   F
He's got the whole world in His hands,
C7   B   F
He's got the whole world in His hands,
C7   B   F
He's got the whole world in His hands,
C7   F
He's got the whole world in His hands.

He's got the little babies in His hands, (3 times)
He's got the whole world in His hands.

He's got you and me, brother, in His hands,
He's got you and me, sister, in His hands,
He's got you and me, brother, in His hands,
He's got the whole world in His hands.

He's got the gamblin' man in His hands, (3 times)
He's got the whole world in His hands.

He's got the whole world in His hands, (4 times)

Ninety And Nine
Elizabeth C. Clephane and Ira D. Sankey

F
There were ninety and nine that safely lay
    Bb   F
In the shelter of the fold,
    Bb   F
But one was out on the hills away,
    C
Far off from the gates of gold.
  F
Away on the mountains wild and bare,
Bb   F
Away from the tender Shepherd's care,
  C7   F
Away from the tender Shepherd's care.

"Lord, Thou hast here Thy ninety and nine;
Are they not enough for Thee?"
But the Shepherd made an answer: "This of nine
Has wandered away from me,
And although the road be rough and steep,
I go to the desert to find my sheep." (twice)

But all through the mountains thunder-riven,
And up from the rocky steep,
There rose a glad cry to the gate of heaven,
"Rejoice, I have found my sheep!"
And the angels echoed around the throne,
"Rejoice, for the Lord brings back his own!" (twice)

Lonesome Valley

A
You got to walk that lonesome valley,
    E7   A
You got to go there by yourself,
      D   A
Ain't nobody here can go there for you,
    B7   A   E7   A
You got to go there by yourself.

If you cannot preach like Peter,
If you cannot pray like Paul,
You can tell the love of Jesus,
You can say He died for all.

Your mother's got to walk that lonesome valley,
She's got to go there by herself,
Ain't nobody else can go there for her,
She's got to go there by herself.

Your father's got to walk that lonesome valley, etc.

Your brother's got to walk that lonesome valley, etc.

Kum Ba Yah (Come By Here)

        C   F   C
Kum ba yah, my Lord, Kum ba yah!
        C   F   G
Kum ba yah, my Lord, Kum ba yah!
        C   F   C
Kum ba yah, my Lord, Kum ba yah!
F C   G7   C
O Lord, Kum ba yah.

Someone's crying, Lord, Kum ba yah!, etc.

Someone's singing, Lord, Kum ba yah!, etc.

Someone's praying, Lord, Kum ba yah!, etc.

Just A Closer Walk With Thee

C   G7
Just a closer walk with Thee,
                C
Grant it Jesus if you please;
  C7   F
Daily walkin' close to Thee,
    C   G   C
Let it be, dear Lord, let it be.

Through the days of toil that's near,
If I fall, dear Lord, who cares?
Who with me my burden share,
None but Thee, dear Lord, none but Thee.

When my feeble life is o'er,
Time for me will be no more;
Guide me gently, safely on,
To Thy shore, dear Lord, to Thy shore.

91

Onward Christian Soldiers

Sabine Baring-Gould and Sir Arthur Sullivan

```
C        G      G7        C
Onward Christian soldiers, marching as to war,
         G    D7    G
With the cross of Jesus going on before.
G7                        C
Christ, the royal Master, leads against the foe;
                                    G7
Forward into battle see His banners go.
```

Chorus:
```
C            G7              C
Onward Christian soldiers, marching as to war,
     G7   C   F D7 G7  C
With the cross of Jesus going on before.
```

```
            G7
Like a mighty army, moves the Church of God,
Brothers, we are treading where the Saints have trod;
We are not divided, all one body we,
One in hope and doctrine, one in charity.
```

Crowns and thrones may perish, kingdoms rise and wane,
But the Church of Jesus constant will remain;
Gates of Hell can never 'gainst that Church prevail,
We have Christ's own promise, and that can never fail.

Onward, then, ye people, join our happy throng,
Blend with ours your voices in the triumph song;
Glory, laud and honor unto Christ the King,
This through countless ages, men and angels sing.

Old Ship Of Zion

```
D      F#m     G      D
What ship is this that will take us all home?
G      A7   DGD
O glory hallelujah!
A7   D    F#min    G      D
And safely land us on Canaan's bright shores?
G      A7   DGD
O glory hallelujah!
```

Chorus:
```
A        D      G
'Tis the old ship of Zion,
     F#m7 Bm7
Hallelu,      hallelu,
         D7      G
'Tis the old ship of Zion,
A7   DGD
Hallelujah!
```

Nobody Knows The Trouble I've Seen

Chorus:
```
F        Bb      F
Nobody knows the trouble I've seen,
     Bb      F
Nobody knows but Jesus.
     Bb      F
Nobody knows the trouble I've seen,
     C7   F
Glory hallelujah!
```

Verses:
```
F
Sometimes I'm up, sometimes I'm down, Oh, yes, Lord!
F                                  C7   F
Sometimes I'm almost to the ground, oh, yes, Lord!
```

```
F
Now, you may think that I don't know,
But I've had my troubles here below, etc.
```

One day when I was walkin' along,
The sky opened up and love came down.

What make old Satan hate me so?
He had me once and had to let me go.

I never shall forget that day,
When Jesus washed my sins away.

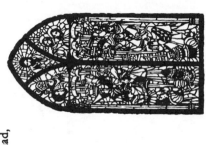

Revive Us Again

William Porter Mackay and John J. Husband

F   Bb   F
We praise Thee, Oh God!
   Bb F
For the Son of Thy love,
     Bb
For Jesus who died
F   C7
And is now gone above.

Refrain:

F   C7   F
Hallelujah! Thine the glory,
     C7
Hallelujah, amen!
F A7 Dm
Hallelujah! Thine the glory,
F Bb F C7F
Revive us again!

We praise Thee, Oh God!
For Thy Spirit of light,
Who has shown us our Savior
And scattered our night.

All glory and praise
To the Lamb that was slain,
Who has borne all our sins
And hath cleansed every stain.

Revive us again;
Fill each heart with Thy love;
May each soul be rekindled
With fire from above.

Rock-A My Soul

 F   C7
Oh, rock-a my soul in the bosom of Abraham,

Rock-a my soul in the bosom of Abraham,
F   C7
Rock-a my soul in the bosom of Abraham,
       F
Oh, rock-a my soul.

Verses:

                 C7
When I went down in the valley to pray,

Oh, rock-a my soul.
 F   C7
My soul got happy and I stayed all day,
       F
Oh, rock-a my soul.

When I was a mourner just like you,
Oh, rock-a my soul,
I mourned and mourned till I come through,
Oh, rock-a my soul.

The Seven Blessings Of Mary

 D
The very first blessing that Mary had,
         A7
It was the blessing of one,
 D   A7
To know that her son, Jesus,
D   A7
Was God's only Son,
G   D
Was God's only Son.

Chorus:

D
Come all ye to the wilderness,
A7   D
Glory, glory, be,
         G   D
Father, Son and the Holy Ghost,
     A7   D
Through all eternity.

The second blessing that Mary had,
It was the blessing of two,
To know that her son, Jesus,
Could read the Bible through. (twice)

The very next blessing that Mary had,
It was the blessing of three,
To know that her son, Jesus,
Could make the blind to see. (twice)

The very next blessing that Mary had,
It was the blessing of four,
To know that her son, Jesus,
Would live to help the poor. (twice)

Sinner Man

Dm
Oh, sinner man, where you gonna run to?
C
Oh, sinner man, where you gonna run to?
Dm
Oh, sinner man, where you gonna run to?
Am   Dm
All on that day?

Run to the rock,
The rock was a-melting (3 times)
All on that day.

Run to the sea,
The sea was a-boiling, etc.

Run to the moon,
The moon was a-bleeding, etc.

Run to the Lord,
Lord won't you hide me? etc.

Oh, sinner man,
You oughta been a-praying, etc.

Sowing On The Mountain

G
Sowing on the mountain, reaping in the valley;

F
Sowing on the mountain, reaping in the valley;
C
Sowing on the mountain, reaping in the valley,
G   D7   G
You're gonna reap just what you sow.

God gave Noah the rainbow sign (3 times)
It won't be water, but fire next time.

Won't be water, but fire next time (3 times)
God gave Noah the rainbow sign.

Streets Of Glory

E
I'm gonna walk the Streets of Glory,
A   E7
I'm gonna walk the Streets of Glory,
E
I'm gonna walk the Streets of Glory,
B7   E
Walk the Streets of Glory one of these days.

One of these days, hallelujah,
One of these days, hallelujah,
I'm gonna tell God how you treat me,
Tell God how you treat me one of these days.

I'm gonna tell God how you treat me, (twice)

Steal Away

Chorus:

F
Steal away, steal away,
C7   F
Steal away to Jesus.

F
Steal away, steal away home,
C7   F
I ain't got long to stay here.

Verses:

Dm   F
My Lord calls me,

He calls me by the thunder,
The trumpet sounds within-a my soul;
C7   F
I ain't got long to stay here.

Green trees are bending,
Poor sinner stands a-trembling,
The trumpet sounds within-a my soul,
I ain't got long to stay here.

Tombstones are bursting,
Poor sinner stands a-trembling, etc.

My Lord calls me,
He calls me by the lightning, etc.

I'm gonna walk and talk with Jesus, etc.

Swing Low, Sweet Chariot

Chorus:

    E
Swing low, sweet chariot,

  A   E
Coming for to carry me home,

     B7
Swing low, sweet chariot,

  A   E
Coming for to carry me home.

Verses:

        A   E
I looked over Jordan and what did I see?

         B7
Coming for to carry me home.

C#m   A   E
A band of angels coming after me,

C#m   A6 B7 E
Coming for to carry me home.

If you get there, before I do, etc.
Tell all my friends, I'm coming too., etc.

Walk In Jerusalem, Just Like John

Chorus:

E
I want to be ready,

A   E
I want to be ready,

     B7 E
I want to be ready,

   E   A   E A E
To walk in Jerusalem just like John.

Verses:

E
John said the city was just four square,

    A   E   A E
Walk in Jerusalem, just like John,

And he declared he'd meet me there,

    F#m A B7 E
Walk in Jerusalem just like john.

Oh, John, Oh, John, what do you say? Walk, etc.
That I'll be there in the coming day, Walk, etc.

When Peter was preaching at Pentacost,
He was endowed with the Holy Ghost,

Wayfaring Stranger

Em   B7   Em
I'm just a poor wayfaring stranger,

          Am   B
A-traveling through this world of woe;

       Em   B7   Em
But there's no sickness no toil nor danger,

          A   Am Bm   Em
In that bright world to which I go.

               Am
I'm going there to see my father,

     Em C   D   G
I'm going there no more to roam,

         B7 Em
I'm just a-going over Jordan,

       A Am Bm Em
I'm just a-going over home.

I know dark clouds will gather 'round me,
I know my way is steep and rough,
But beauteous fields lie just beyond me,
Where souls redeemed their vigil keep.
I'm going there to meet my mother,
She said she'd meet me when I come;
I'm only going over Jordan,
I'm only going over home.

I want to wear a crown of glory,
When I get home to that bright land;
I want to shout Salvation's story,
In concert with that bloodwashed band.
I'm going there to meet my Saviour,
To sing His praises for evermore;
I'm only going over Jordan,
I'm only going over home.

What A Friend We Have In Jesus

Joseph Scriven and Charles C. Converse

Bb
What a friend we have in Jesus,
F   **Eb**
All our sins and griefs to bear!
F
What a privilege to carry
F   **Eb**
Ev'rything to God in prayer!
F   **Bb**
Oh what peace we often forfeit,
Eb
Oh what needless pain we bear,
Eb
All because we do not carry

F
Ev'rything to God in prayer!

Bb
Have we trials and temptations?
Is there trouble anywhere?
We should never be discouraged,
Take it to the Lord in prayer.
Can we find a friend so faithful
Who will all our sorrows share?
Jesus knows our ev'ry weakness,
Take it to the Lord in prayer.

Are we weak and heavy laden,
Cumbered with a load of care?
Precious Savior, still our refuge,
Take it to the Lord in prayer.
Do thy friends despise, forsake thee?
Take it to the Lord in prayer;
In His arms He'll take and shield thee,
Thou wilt find a solace there.

Were You There When They Crucified My Lord?

F   **Bb C7**   **Bb**
Were you there when they crucified my Lord?
F   **Am**   **Bb Am Bb C**
Were you there when they crucified my Lord?
Dm Am   Dm F7 Bb   F   Gm Am
O sometimes it causes me to tremble, tremble, tremble;
Dm   BbmF   **Bb Am C7 Bb**
Were you there when they crucified my Lord?

Were you there when they nailed Him to the tree? (twice)
O sometimes it causes me to tremble, tremble, tremble;
Were you there when they nailed Him to the tree?

Were you there when they pierced Him in the side?, etc.

Were you there when the sun refused to shine?, etc.

Were you there when they laid Him in the tomb?, etc.

When The Saints Go Marching In

F
Oh, when the Saints go marching in,
                                          C7
Oh, when the Saints go marching in,
F   F7   Bb
Lord, I want to be in that number,
F   **C7 F**
When the Saints go marching in.

And when the revelation comes, etc.

Oh, when the new world is revealed, etc.

Oh, when they gather 'round the throne, etc.

And when they crown him King of Kings, etc.

And when the sun no more will shine, etc.

And when the moon has turned to blood, etc.

And on that hallelujah day, etc.

And when the earth has turned to fire, etc.

Oh, when the Saints go marching in, etc.

SONGS
of the
HOLIDAYS

Away In A Manger

F   Bb
Away in a manger, no crib for a bed,
     C7   F
The little Lord Jesus lay down his sweet head.
               Bb   F
The stars in the sky looked down where he lay,
 C7   F   Bb   C7 F
The little Lord Jesus, asleep on the hay.

The cattle are lowing, the baby awakes,
But little Lord Jesus, no crying he makes.
I love thee, Lord Jesus, look down from the sky,
And stay by my cradle till morning is nigh.

Be near me, Lord Jesus, I ask thee to stay
Close by me forever, and love me, I pray.
Bless all the dear children in thy tender care,
And fit us for heaven to live with thee there.

Auld Lang Syne
Robert Burns

    F   C7
Should auld acquaintance be forgot,
  F   Bb
And never brought to mind?
    F   C7
Should auld acquaintance be forgot,
  F   C7 F
And days of auld lang syne?

Chorus:

    F   C7
For auld lang syne, my dear
  F   Bb
For auld lang syne
     F   C7
We'll take a cup o' kindness yet,
  F C7 F
For auld lang syne.

Angels We Have Heard On High

F   C7   F
Angels we have heard on high,
   CF   C7 F
Sweetly singing o'er the plains;
    Dm C   F C7 Dm
And the mountains in reply
F C F   C7 F
Echoing their joyous strains.

Refrain:

Bb CF CF Bb F C
Gloria in excelsis Deo,
Bb CF CF Bb F C7 F
Gloria in excelsis Deo.

Shepherds, why this jubilee?
Why your joyous songs prolong?
What the gladsome tidings be
Which inspire your heav'nly song?

Come to Bethlehem and see
Him whose birth the angels sing;
Come adore on bended knee
Christ, the Lord, our new-born King.

Chanuke, O Chanuke

Yiddish

Em
Chanuke, O Chanuke, a yontev a sheyner,

       Am Em
A lustiger, a freylicher, nite noch a zoyner!

          Am Em
Ale nacht in dreydl shpiln mir,

          Am Em
Zudigheyse latkes esn mir.

Chorus:

Em
Geshivinder, tsindt kinder,

      Am   Em
Di dininke lichtelech on.

    Am   Em   Am
Zogt "Alhanisim," loybt Got far di nisim,

    Em   Am   Em
Un kumt gichertaersn in kon!

Yehuda hot fartribn dem soyne, dem rotseyach,
Un hot in Beys-hamikdesh gezungen "Lamnatseyach",
Di shtot Yerusholayim hot vider oyfgelebt,
Un tsu a nayem lebn hot yederer geshtrebt.

Second Chorus:
Deriber, dem giber,
Yehuda Makabi loybt hoych!
Zol yeder bazunder, bazingen di vunder,
Un libn dos folk zolt ir oych!

Singable Translation:

Chanukah, O Chanukah, O holiday so fair,
So happy and so merry, there's none can compare.
We spin the dreydl-top every night,
Red-hot pancakes do we eat.

Maccabee defeated and cast out the cruel enemy,
And in the Holy Temple sang hymns of victory,
The city of Jerusalem revived and grew,
And everyone began to build his life anew.

Come children, we'll light
The thin, little candles you see,
For the salvation of a grateful nation,
Thank God and dance merrily!

Come children prepare for
A real tribute to the Maccabee.
Let us all sing of the victory
And a people so brave and so free.

98

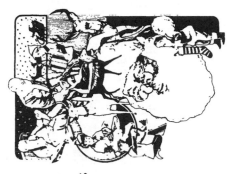

The First Noel

```
        D    A G D   G D
The first Noel the angels did say
G      D   G   D  G  A D     A7  D
Was to certain poor shepherds in fields as they lay;
A7  D     A  G  D    G    G D
In  fields where they lay keeping their sheep
G    G    D   G A   D   A7 D
On a cold winter's night   that was so   deep.
```

Chorus:

```
A7 Bm    A D G    D
No-el, No-el, No-el, No-el,
Bm  F#m G  D   G A7 D A7D
Born is    the king   of Is-ra-el.
```

They looked up and saw a star
Shining in the East, beyond them far,
And to the earth it gave great light,
And so it continued, both day and night.

And by the light of that same star
Three wise men came from country far,
To seek for a King was their intent,
And to follow the star wherever it went.

This star drew night to the northwest;
O'er Bethlehem it took its rest.
And there it did both stop and stay,
Right over the place where Jesus lay.

Then they did know assuredly
Within that house, the King did lie
One entered in then for to see
And found the babe in poverty.

Then entered in those Wise Men three,
Full reverently, upon bended knee,
And offered there, in His presence,
Their gold and myrrh and frankincense.

If we in our time do will
We shall be free from death and hell
For God hath prepared for us all
A resting place in general.

Deck The Halls

```
E          B     E
Deck the halls with boughs of holly,
A     E    B7 E
Fa la la la, la la la  la.
E      B     E
'Tis the season to be jolly,
A     E    B7 E
Fa la la la, la la la  la.
B          E        B
Don we now our gay apparel,
E    C#m  B F#7 B
Fa la la, la la la    la.
E      B    E
Troll the ancient Yuletide carol,
A     E    B7 E
Fa la la la, la la la  la.
```

See the blazing yule before us, Fa la, etc.
Strike the harp and join the chorus, Fa la, etc.
Follow me in merry measure, Fa la, etc.
While I tell of Christmas treasure, Fa la, etc.

Fast away the old year passes,
Hail the new, ye lads and lasses,
Sing we joyous all together,
Heedless of the wind and weather,

Go Tell It On The Mountain

```
G          Em7 Em
When I was a learner,
Am7    D         D7 G
I   sought   both night and day,
               Em7 Em
I asked the Lord to help  me,
Am7    Am              D
And He showed me the way.
```

Chorus:

```
G
Go tell it on the mountain;
D                      D7
Over the hills and ev'ry where;
                Em
Go tell it on the mountain,
Am7 G    D    D7 G
Our  Jesus Christ is  born.
```

```
While shepherds kept their watching;
O'er wand'ring flock by night;
Behold! From out the Heavens,
There shone a holy light.
```

```
He made me a watchman
Upon the city wall,
And if I am a Christian
I am the least of all.
```

```
And, lo, when they had seen it,
They all bowed down and prayed;
Then travelled on together,
To where the Babe was laid.
```

God Rest You Merry Gentlemen

```
A7  Dm     A7   Dm
God rest you merry gentlemen,
F   Gm              A
Let nothing you dismay;
A7Dm      A7       Dm
Remember Christ our Saviour
F    Gm            A
Was born on Christmas Day;
     Bb          F
To save us all from Satan's power
      Dm           C
When we were gone astray.
```

Refrain:

```
         F       A7      Dm
Oh tidings of comfort and joy,
                 C
Comfort and joy,
              A7           Dm
Oh tidings of comfort and joy.
```

```
'Twas in the town of Bethlehem
This blessed infant lay;
They found him in a manger
Where oxen feed on hay;
His mother Mary kneeling
Unto the Lord did pray.
Oh, tidings of comfort and joy,
Comfort and joy,
Oh,tidings of comfort and joy.
```

```
Now to the Lord sing praises,
All you within this place;
And with true love and brotherhood
Each other now embrace;
God bless your friends and kindred
That live both far and near,
And God send you a happy New Year!
Happy New Year!
And God send you a happy New Year!
```

Good King Wenceslas

G
Good King Wenceslas looked out
C   G   C   D7 G
On the feast of   Stephen,

When the snow lay 'round about
C   G   C   D7 G
Deep and crisp and even.
    C G   D7 G   D7 Em
Brightly shone the moon that night,
C   G   C   D7 G
Though the frost was cruel,
      C   D7 Em   D
When a poor man came in sight,
G   D7 G D7Em C G
Gath'ring winter fu -   el.

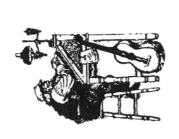

"Hither page, and stand by me,
If thou know'st it, telling,
Yonder peasant who is he?
Where and what his dwelling?"
"Sire, he lives a good league hence,
Underneath the mountains;
Right against the forest fence,
By Saint Agnes' fountain."

"Bring me flesh and bring me wine,
Bring me pine logs hither.
Thou and I will see him dine
When we bear them thither."
Page and monarch, forth they went,
Forth they went together,
Through the rude winds wild lament,
And the bitter weather.

"Sire, the night is darker now,
And the wind blows stronger.
Fails my heart, I know not how
I can go no longer."
"Mark my footsteps, my good page,
Tread thou in them boldly;
Thou shalt find the winter's rage
Freeze thy blood less coldly."

Hark! The Herald Angels Sing
Charles Wesley and Felix Mendelssohn

G   G   G   D
Hark! the herald angels sing,
G   G   G D7 G
Glory to the new-born King;
G   D   Emin A7
Peace on earth and mercy mild,
Bmin D   G7A7D
God and sinners reconciled!
G   D
Joyful all ye nations rise,
G   D
Join the triumph of the skies;
C   Amin E7 Amin
With angelic host   proclaim,
D7   G   G   D7G
Christ is born in Bethlehem.

Chorus:

C   E   Amin
Hark! the herald angels sing,
D7   G   D7 G
Glory to the new-born King.

Christ, by highest heav'n adored;
Christ, the everlasting Lord;
Late in time behold Him come,
Offspring of the Virgin's womb.
Veil'd in flesh the Godhead see;
Hail th' Incarnate Deity,
Pleased as Man with man to dwell,
Jesus, our Emmanuel!

Mild He lays His glory by,
Born that man no more may die,
Born to raise the sons of earth,
Born to give them second birth.
Ris'n with healing in His wings,
Light and life to all He brings,
Hail, the Sun of Righteousness!
Hail, the heav'n born Prince of Peace!

Season's Greetings

101

Jingle Bells
J. S. Pierpont

G
Dashing through the snow

In a one-horse open sleigh,
    D7
O'er the fields we go,
    G
Laughing all the way;

Bells on bob-tail ring,
    C
Making spirits bright;
    D7
What fun it is to ride and sing
    G
A sleighing song tonight!

Chorus:

G
Jingle bells! Jingle bells!

Jingle all the way!
C   G
Oh what fun it is to ride
   A7
In a one-horse open sleigh.
D7 G   D
Oh! Jingle bells! Jingle bells!

Jingle all the way!
C   G
Oh what fun it is to ride
   D7   G
In a one-horse open sleigh.

A day or two ago
I thought I'd take a ride,
And soon Miss Fannie Bright
Was seated by my side;
The horse was lean and lank,
Misfortune seem'd his lot,
He got into a drifted bank,
And then we got upsot!

Joy To The World
Isaac Watts / Tune: adapted from
Handel's Messiah by Lowell Mason

D G   D   G D   A D
Joy to the world, the Lord is come;
 G   A7   D
Let Earth receive her King;
     G   D   G   D
Let every heart prepare Him room,

And Heaven and nature sing,
   A7
And Heaven and nature sing,
    D   G   D   G DA7 D
And Heaven and Heaven and nature sing!

Joy to the world! the Savior reigns.
Let men their songs employ,
While fields and floods,
Rocks, hills and plains
Repeat the sounding joy, (twice)
Repeat, repeat, the sounding joy.

He rules the world with truth and grace,
And makes the nations prove
The glories of
His righteousness,
And wonders of His love, (twice)
And wonders, wonders, of His love.

Mi Y'Malel
(Who Can Retell?)
Hebrew; Chanukah Song

E
Mi Y'malel g'vurot Yisrael,

Otan mi yimneh?

Hen bekhol dor yakum hagibor,
    C#mE
Goel haam.
Bm B Em   F#   Bm
Sh'ma! Bayamim hahem baz'mam hazzeh
Em F#   Bm B
Makabi moshia ufodeh.
Em   F#   B Bm
Uv'yamenu kol am Yisrael.
G   F#   Em
Yitahed, yakum veyigael.

Singable Translation:

Who can retell the things that befell us,
Who can count them?
In every age a hero or sage
Came to our aid.
Hark! At this time of year
In days of yore,
Maccabees the Temple did restore.
But now all Israel must as one rise,
Redeem itself through deed and sacrifice.

B

O, Come, All Ye Faithful

G   D   G D G   G D G   C G D
O, come all ye faithful, joyful and triumphant,
Em   D A D   G D   A D
O, come ye, O, come ye to Bethlehem;
G   D7 G Am G   D   G Em Am D
Come and behold him, born the king of   angels;

Chorus:

G   D G D7G
O, come, let us adore him
       D G D7G D
O, come, let us adore him
G D7 G D7 A7D G   Am
O, come, let us   adore him
G   D7 G
Christ, the Lord!

Sing chorus of angels, sing in exultation
O, sing all ye citizens of heaven above!
Glory to God, all glory in the highest;

Yea Lord, we greet thee, born this happy morning
Jesus, to thee be all glory giv'n:
Word of the father. Now in flesh appearing;

Latin:

Adeste, fideles,
Laeti triumphantes,
Venite, venite in Bethlehem.
Natum videte,
Regem angelorum,
Venite, adoremus,
Venite, adoremus,
Venite, adoremus Dominum.

103

Oh, Little Town Of Bethlehem
Philip Brooks and Lewis H. Redner

    G   Am
Oh little town of Bethlehem,
    G   D7   G
How still we see thee lie,
    E7   Am
Above thy deep and dreamless sleep
    G   D7   G
The silent stars go by;
    Adim7 A# dim7 B
Yet in thy dark streets shineth
    Em C   B
The everlasting light,
    G   Am
The hopes and fears of all the years,
    G   D7   G
Are met in thee tonight.

For Christ is born of Mary,
And gathered all above,
While mortals sleep, the angels keep
Their watch of wondering love.
Oh morning stars, together
Proclaim the holy birth,
And praises sing to God the King,
And peace to men on earth.

Oh holy Child of Bethlehem!
Descend to us, we pray;
Cast out the sin and enter in,
Be born in us today.
We hear the Christmas angels
The great glad tidings tell;
Oh come to us, abide with us,
Our Lord Immanuel!

104

Silent Night
Joseph Mohr and Franz Gruber

C
Silent night, Holy night,
G7   C
All is calm, all is bright,
F   C
Round yon Virgin Mother and Child,
F   C
Holy Infant so tender and mild,
G7   Am
Sleep in heavenly peace,
C   G7   C
Sleep in heavenly peace.

Silent night, Holy night,
Shepherds quake at the sight;
Glories stream from heaven afar,
Heavenly hosts sing alleluia,
Christ, the Savior, is born! (twice)

Silent night, Holy night,
Son of God, love's pure light
Radiant beams from Thy holy face,
With the dawn of redeeming grace,
Jesus, Lord at Thy birth, (twice)

How silently, how silently
The wondrous gift is given!
So God imparts to human hearts
The blessings of His heaven.
No ear may hear His coming,
But in this world of sin,
Where meek souls will receive Him still,
The dear Christ enters in.

The Twelve Days Of Christmas

```
      F      Bb        C7              F
On the first day of Christmas my true love gave to me
Bb   F   C7  F
A partridge in a pear tree.
     F       Dm          C7                      F
On the second day of Christmas my true love gave to me
C     F     Bb    F   C7  F
Two turtle doves and a partridge in a pear tree.
     F      C         Gm
On the third day . . . three French hens
     F       C       Gm
On the fourth day . . . four colly birds
     F        Dm G7 C7
On the fifth day . . . five golden rings.
F    Gm Bb    Dm G      C
Four colly birds, three French hens, two turtle doves,
F     Bb      C7  F
And a partridge in a pear tree.
C7     Gm7
Six geese a-laying, etc.
```

Seven swans a-swimming, etc.

Eight maids a-milking, etc.

Nine ladies dancing, etc.

Ten lords a-leaping, etc.

Eleven pipers piping, etc.

Twelve drummers drumming, etc.

Wassail Song

```
D    Em  F#m  EmDEmF#m
Here we  come  a-wassailing,
EmD      A7      D
Among the leaves so green;
G    A7 D    F#m Em
Here we  come a-wandering,
D G  A7  D
So fair to be seen:
```

Chorus:

```
       D        Bm D
Love and joy come to  you,
Bm  Em D       Bm D
And to  you your wassail, too,
    G  D  Bm   Em D   D  A D    G
And God bless you and send you a  happy New Year,
D  G   A  G  Bm EmD A   D
And God send you a  happy New Year.
```

```
Our wassail cup is made
Of the rosemary tree,
And so is your beer
Of the best barley.
```

```
We are not daily beggars
That beg from door to door,
But we are neighbors' children
Whom you have seen before.
```

```
Call up the butler of this house,
Put on his golden ring,
Let him bring us up a glass of beer,
And better we shall sing.
```

```
We have got a little purse
Of stretching leather skin;
We want a little of your money
To line it well within.
```

```
Bring us out a table,
And spread it with a cloth;
Bring us out mouldy cheese,
And some of your Christmas loaf.
```

```
God bless the master of this house,
Likewise the mistress, too;
And all the little children
That round the table go.
```

I Saw Three Ships Come Sailing In

```
G              D
I saw three ships come sailing in
C  G           D
On Christmas Day, on Christmas Day,
G              Bm   D
I saw three ships come sailing in
C  G       D    G
On Christmas Day in the morning.
```

And what was in those ships all three
On Christmas Day, on Christmas Day?
And what was in those ships all three
On Christmas Day in the morning?

The mother Mary and her baby, etc.

Pray, whither sailed those ships all three, etc.

Oh, they sailed into Bethlehem, etc.

And all the bells on earth shall ring, etc.

And all the angels in Heaven shall sing, etc.

And all the souls on earth shall sing, etc.

Then let us all rejoice amain, etc.

We Wish You A Merry Christmas

```
E              A
We wish you a Merry Christmas,
F#             B7
We wish you a Merry Christmas,
C#m            A
We wish you a Merry Christmas,
B7             E
And a Happy New Year.
```

We want some figgy pudding, (3 times)
And a cup of good cheer!

We won't go until we get some, (3 times)
So bring it out here!

We wish you a Merry Christmas, (3 times)
And a Happy New Year!

What Child Is This?

William C. Dix / Tune: Greensleeves

```
Em             D
What Child is this, who laid to rest,
Em    C    B7
On Mary's lap is sleeping?
Em             D
Who angels greet with anthems sweet,
Em    B7   Em
While shepherds watch are keeping?
```

Refrain:
```
G              D
This, this is Christ the King,
Em    C    B7
Whom shepherds guard and angels sing;
G              D
Haste, haste to Bring Him laud,
Em    B7   Em
The Babe, the Son of Mary.
```

Why lies He in such mean estate,
Where ox and ass are feeding?
Good Christian fear, for sinners here,
The silent word is pleading?

So bring Him incense, gold and myrrh,
Come peasant kind, to own Him.
The Kind of kings salvation brings,
Let loving hearts enthrone him.

Favorite 19th Century American Songs for Fingerstyle Guitar

by Glenn Weiser

This is a collection of 47 favorite 19th century American songs arranged for fingerstyle guitar from Glenn Weiser's recent CD, *My Old Kentucky Home.*

Here you'll find Stephen Foster's famous compositions and other parlor songs, African-American spirituals, Civil War anthems, familiar hymns and 1890s hits. Now guitarists can play these songs in new, beautiful solo arrangements.

00291915 Book/Online Audio................ $24.99

(EAN 978-1-57424-379-6) (UPC 8-88680-92836-0)

ASAP Beginning Bluegrass Banjo
LEARN HOW TO PLAY THE BLUEGRASS WAY
by Ron Middlebrook with Dick Sheridan

Here's a surefire way to get going and learn how to play the 5-string banjo bluegrass style! Detailed tips and explanations provide help and understanding of the fundamentals and how to apply them to make you a great banjo player. Topics covered include: tuning • reading tablature • basic rolls • intros, breaks, fills & tags • 30 bluegrass songs • and much more. Includes access to audio tracks online for download or streaming.

00295683 Book/Online Audio $14.99
(EAN 978-1-57424-381-9)
(UPC 8-88680-94860-3)